BACKGROUND TO THE BIBLE

BACKGROUND TO THE BIBLE

AN INTRODUCTION TO SCRIPTURE STUDY

Richard T. A. Murphy, O.P.

Servant Books
Ann Arbor, Michigan

Nihil Obstat: Rev. Robert Lunsford
Imprimatur: Most Reverend Kenneth Povish
               Bishop of Lansing

Published by Servant Books
               Box 8617
               Ann Arbor, Michigan 48107
Available from Servant Publications
               Distribution Center
               237 North Michigan
               South Bend, Indiana 46601

Front cover photo: Tenth century A. D. manuscript showing a portion of the Hebrew Pentateuch. Courtesy of The University of Michigan Library, Department of Rare Books and Special Collections.

Printed in the United States of America
ISBN 0-89283-055-7

CONTENTS

CHARTS AND ILLUSTRATIONS

Abbreviations of the Books of the Bible

OLD TESTAMENT

Am	Amos	2 Kgs	2 Kings
Bar	Baruch	Lam	Lamentations
1 Chr	1 Chronicles	Lv	Leviticus
2 Chr	2 Chronicles	Mal	Malachi
Dn	Daniel	1 Mc	1 Maccabees
Dt	Deuteronomy	2 Mc	2 Maccabees
Est	Esther	Mi	Micah
Ex	Exodus	Na	Nahum
Ez	Ezekiel	Neh	Nehemiah
Ezr	Ezra	Nm	Numbers
Gn	Genesis	Ob	Obadiah
Hb	Habakkuk	Prv	Proverbs
Hg	Haggai	Ps	Psalms
Hos	Hosea	Qo	Qoheleth
Is	Isaiah	Ru	Ruth
Jb	Job	Sg	Song of Songs
Jdt	Judith	Sir	Sirach
Jer	Jeremiah	1 Sm	1 Samuel
Jgs	Judges	2 Sm	2 Samuel
Jl	Joel	Tb	Tobit
Jon	Jonah	Wis	Wisdom
Jos	Joshua	Zec	Zechariah
1 Kgs	1 Kings	Zep	Zephaniah

NEW TESTAMENT

Acts	Acts of the Apostles	Mk	St. Mark
Col	Colossians	Mt	St. Matthew
1 Cor	1 Corinthians	Phil	Philippians
2 Cor	2 Corinthians	Phlm	Philemon
Eph	Ephesians	1 Pt	1 St. Peter
Gal	Galatians	2 Pt	2 St. Peter
Heb	Hebrews	Rom	Romans
Jas	St. James	Rv	Revelation
Jn	St. John	1 Thes	1 Thessalonians
1 Jn	1 St. John	2 Thes	2 Thessalonians
2 Jn	2 St. John	Ti	Titus
3 Jn	3 St. John	1 Tm	1 Timothy
Jude	St. Jude	2 Tm	2 Timothy
Lk	St. Luke		

INTRODUCTION

The Bible enjoys an extraordinary reputation. Everybody wants to have it on his side, or to be on its side. A recent Gallup poll revealed that in America, an astonishing number of people (83 percent) believe that the Bible is the word of God. If that is true, it is obviously an important book, and deserves all the attention it gets.

In bygone days, a large Bible occupied a table in front parlors in many Christian homes. Clamps held the thick covers tightly shut. The book was a convenient place for family records, and was of proven excellence for pressing flowers, but it was not often read. It was an unknown book, and still is. St. John Chrysostom once lamented the fact that some people did not know how many letters St. Paul had written! Things have changed some, but there are still those who do not know where they can find the book of Genesis, and others who think the letter to the Hebrews was written in Hebrew, and the one to the Romans in Latin! Some have thought that Dan and Beersheba, two towns, were husband and wife.

The study of the Bible is a life-long work. Enormous amounts of information must be absorbed, with the result that an introduction to the Bible might seem to the beginner to be too formidable and somewhat disorganized. It is not. It is just that the matter is so complicated, and may seem to be repetitious at times. Actually, as the tide comes in, each wave reaches a bit farther on to the shore, and in much the same way our repetitions mark progress. One cannot say everything at once. But to obviate difficulties, numerous headings will appear in the text to help the reader keep his bearings.

Captain Joshua Slocum, the first man ever to sail alone around the world, once observed, with typical New England shrewdness, that "all a sailor asks of the sea is permission to sail his ship." No sea-going man would dream of asking for winds and tides that were always favorable, or seas that were ever-smooth. A sailor can cope with such difficulties, and reach his destinations in spite of them. Biblical voyages are likewise not without difficulties, but they too can be coped with. The goal—a better understanding of the word of God—can be attained with a reasonable expenditure of energy and skill.

The study of the Bible is unfortunately linked, in the minds of many, with destructive criticism. Many fear that the scholars, who seem to speak a strange, technical jargon, are secretly determined to pass judgment, and an unfavorable one, on God's word. But this is to overlook the very nature of criticism, which is the art of estimating the qualities and character of a literary or artistic work. Biblical criticism is something like music or art or literary criticism; when properly conducted, it leads to a better understanding and appreciation. A rational approach is not for that reason necessarily an irreverent one, but in fact adds a healthy dimension to piety.

It has been accurately said that one gets out of a trip pretty much what he brings with him. The better one's background—the more he knows about the history and art and literature and culture of another land—the more he will appreciate its treasures when he sees the land that produced them. Much the same can be said about reading the Bible. If one approaches it with some knowledge of history, form criticism, midrash, mythology, theology, languages, and so on, the greater the dividends such knowledge will bring him.

This book, it is hoped, will help people read and appreciate the Bible, not as an ancient classic (although it is that), but as a source of inspiration and guidance. St. Paul assured Timothy that "the word of God can profitably be used for teaching, for refuting error, for guiding people's lives, and teaching them to be holy." That is a strong recommendation for reading on.

The Bible revolves about a majestic, incredibly magnificent, and wholly breathtaking theme—God's loving plan for the salvation of man. Man's response to God's loving overtures has not always been one of love, gratitude, and service. The Bible, a singularly unromantic and unsentimental book, makes that abundantly clear. In its pages there walk many people like ourselves, people who, when faced with crises, sometimes succeed in doing great things, and sometimes fall flat on their faces. The Bible is Everyman's book.

Many want to read the Bible and understand its message, but simply do not know where to start. Few have the background and training to seek it on their own. Some have plunged into a reading of the Bible confident that the Holy Spirit would lead them to the correct understanding of what they read. History has shown how seldom that has happened. The Holy Spirit wants us to use our brains, and if these are not enough, to pick the brains of others, the good biblical scholars. Standing on their shoulders, many will find that these guides are indeed giants, as well as an example and help to others. Reading and interpreting the Bible is not within the range of "Do-it-yourself."

This book is only an introduction. Introductions are important in the business world. It helps to be introduced around, to meet people, to learn the ropes. After that, one is on his own, although in a very true sense a Bible reader is never alone, for the Bible engages him in a never-ending dialogue with God.

Since these pages are written from within the Roman Catholic communion, they will refer from time to time to the various official pronouncements of that Church. By this is meant the various biblical encyclicals and especially the scriptural document issued at Vatican II, the *Dei Verbum*. Official pronouncements are generally accorded a bad press; it will come as a surprise to some, then, that these documents are characterized by common sense and a wholly remarkable breadth of vision.

I would like to add a word of special thanks to James Manney of Servant Books for his skillful editing of the manuscript and many helpful suggestions, and to Frank and Rose Liberto for their assistance in bringing this book into its final shape.

It is now time to heed the good advice given by an ancient author (2 Mc 2:32) and to begin our task without further ado. It would be silly indeed to write a long, long preface, and then have to abbreviate the story itself.

Part One

The Bible Comes Into Being

ONE

WHAT IS THE BIBLE?

The word "Bible" comes from *ta biblia,* the Greek neuter-plural form of *to biblion,* which means book or scroll (2 Mc 8:23; Dn 9:2). The word indicates two things: first, that the Bible is in a class all by itself, a book so important that it needs no other title than "The Book." The Bible is the Book of Books, or the Good Book. Secondly, the plural form suggests that the Bible is not a single work, but a small library of books written by many authors.

People think twice about tackling a large, unfamiliar book, and the Bible is both large and unfamiliar. We can begin to dispel the mystery that surrounds the Bible by learning the lay of the land, that is, the overall divisions of the Old and New Testaments, and the arrangement and contents of the books in each section. The chart provided here shows how the books are arranged, and which books fall under each division. In the Jewish Scriptures the threefold division is: the *Law,* the *Prophets,* and the *Writings.* In a Christian Bible the division is into *historical, didactic,* and *prophetical* books. The terms are broad but useful descriptions of the contents of the books in those categories. Books listed separately in Christian Bibles are sometimes joined together in the Hebrew. There is nothing significant in this, except that the thirty-nine or forty-six books in Protestant or Roman Catholic Bibles become twenty-two books in the He-

OLD TESTAMENT

The Hebrew Scriptures

Torah (Pentateuch)
Genesis
Exodus
Leviticus
Numbers
Deuteronomy

The Prophets

Early
Joshua
Judges
Samuel
Kings

Later
Isaiah
Jeremiah
Ezekiel
The Twelve

The Writings
Psalms
Job & Proverbs
Ruth
Song of Songs & Qoheleth
Lamentations
Esther
Daniel
Ezra & Nehemiah
Chronicles

The Christian Old Testament

The Historical Books
Genesis
Exodus
Leviticus
Numbers
Deuteronomy
Joshua
Judges
Ruth
Samuel
Kings
Chronicles
Ezra
Nehemiah
Tobit
Judith
Esther
Maccabees

The Writings (Wisdom Books)
Job
Psalms
Proverbs
Qoheleth
Song of Songs
Wisdom
Sirach

The Prophets
Isaiah
Jeremiah
Lamentations
Baruch
Ezekiel
Daniel
Hosea
Joel
Amos
Obadiah
Jonah
Micah
Nahum
Habakkuk
Zephaniah
Haggai
Zechariah
Malachi

NEW TESTAMENT

The Historical Books
Matthew
Mark
Luke
John
Acts

Apostolic Letters
Romans
1 Corinthians
2 Corinthians
Galatians
Ephesians
Philippians
Colossians
1-2 Thessalonians
1-2 Timothy
Titus
Philemon
Hebrews

Letters to all Christians
James
1-2 Peter
1-2-3 John
Jude

An Apocalypse
Revelation

brew Scriptures. No one knows quite how to explain this, but it has been observed that in the Hebrew alphabet there are twenty-two letters. There may be a connection.

It is a strange fact that the books of the Bible are not arranged in strict chronological order. Naturally the story of creation and of the patriarchs comes first—Genesis. But from then on, one needs seven-league boots to cope with the leaps through time. Exodus, the second book, introduces Moses and leads up to the happenings at Mt. Sinai. Joshua, Judges, and Samuel bring one to David and Solomon, while Kings and Chronicles, Ezra and Nehemiah tell of the Divided Kingdom, the Exile, and the Return. By the time the story of the Maccabees is finished, one has covered almost two millenia—from about 1850 to 63 B.C.

The Old Testament books come to us without publication dates. In the arrangement of the prophetical section, one sees editorial hands at work. Amos and Micah both preceded Isaiah in time, but it is Isaiah, the first and longest of the major prophets, who heads the others. Isaiah gives many important details about the coming Messiah. (For example, see in Isaiah the "Book of Emmanuel" and also the "Servant Songs.") The minor prophets are put together under the rubric of The Twelve. Such an ordering scheme indicates editorial intervention. It was surely editorial policy to place Joshua, Judges, Samuel, and Kings—books which we consider historical— among the Early (as opposed to the Later) Prophets. Editors also put Daniel, for us a major prophet, among the Writings. But St. Paul (see Rom 1:2) and the early Church regarded as prophets all those Old Testament people who were deemed to have uttered statements that were applicable to Christ.

In Paul's case too, editors have arranged the books in a sort of order. Among Paul's epistles, Romans comes first. This seems reasonable; it is the most important and longest of his letters. The epistle to the Hebrews is also quite long, but it was the object of so much controversy in the early centuries (did Paul write it himself, or did someone else?) that it was put in the last place.

For the benefit of those who would like to read Paul's letters in the order in which they were written, a simple list of probable, but still disputed, dates is given here. Reading his letters in order helps the reader grow with Paul. We can appreciate how his mind worked and how his thought developed over the years.

51	1-2 Thessalonians
55?	Philippians
57	1 Corinthians
	Galatians
	2 Corinthians
58	Romans
61-63	Colossians
	Ephesians?
	Philemon
	Philippians
65?	1 Timothy?
	Titus?
	Hebrews?
	2 Timothy?

Such arrangements do not in the least affect the contents of any of the books just named. It is the books themselves that are important, not the order in which we find them.

The Jewish Scriptures

The Jews do not refer to their sacred writings as "the Bible," an anglicized Greek word. Nor do they have an "Old" Testament. To them, their "book" has never been superseded by a "New" Testament. The Jews describe their holy writings as *Torah, Neviim,* and *Kethuvim,* which mean "Law," "Prophets," and "Writings." Sometimes they refer to it, for short, by the acronym *Tanak* (T-N-K), a simple mnemonic.

The word *Torah* means "Law," and comprises the first five books of the Bible.* The Greek word for them is "Pentateuch," meaning "the five scrolls." Christians refer to these books by Greek or Latin titles: Genesis, Exodus, Leviticus, Numbers, and Deuteronomy. These titles are roughly descriptive of the contents. The Jews, however, identify these books by their opening word or words. Genesis is *bereshith;* Exodus is *weelleh shemoth;* Leviticus is *wayyigra;* Numbers, *wa-yedabber;* Deuteronomy is *elleh haddebarim.* Such a practice is fairly common; papal encyclicals are named by the way they begin. For example, Pius XII's great encyclical on Scripture begins with the words *Divino Afflante Spiritu.*

The second division of the Jewish Scriptures is the section called *Neviim* (the plural of *navi,* prophet). In addition to the sub-title "Early" and "Later," the Jews also sometimes describe the prophets as "Former" (also: "Non-Writing") and "Latter" (also: "Writing") Prophets.

The third section of the Jewish Scriptures is called *Kethuvim* or "Writings," taken from the Hebrew *ktv* or *kathav,* which means "to write." This section contains five books which constitute the "wisdom writings" of the Jews. The word "didactic" is also connected to this type of literature which is found also in Egypt and Mesopotamia. The Jewish "wisdom" books are: the Psalms *(tehillim),* Job, Proverbs *(mishle Shelomoh),* the Song of Songs *(shir-hashshirim),* and Qoheleth (formerly called Ecclesiastes). This section also contains Lamentations, Esther, Daniel, Ezra-Nehemiah, and Chronicles. The books of Wisdom and Sirach (formerly Ecclesiasticus) are lacking in the Jewish Scriptures.

The Christian Bible

Everyman's book, the Bible, is in a special sense associated with the Church. It was the early Church that presided over the

---

*Torah can also stand for the entire revelation embodied in the Old Testament. The Psalms are not legal documents but are regarded as part of the "law" (see Jn 10:34).

birth of the New Testament and accepted it, along with the Old Testament, as faithfully reflecting her faith and her understanding of the relationship which exists between God and man.

The Christian Bible contains two testaments, the Old and the New, each of which is divided into historical, didactic (sometimes called sapiential or wisdom) and prophetic books. The ordering of the sections is different from that of the Jewish book. After the historical section of the Old Testament come the writings, and in third place, almost as if they were peering in the direction of the New Testament, come the prophets. The historical books of the New Testament are the gospels and Acts; the didactic books are the letters of Paul and the other letters; last is the Apocalypse or Revelation, the only book of prophetical writing in the New Testament. More will be said about the additional Old Testament books of the Christian Bible in Chapter Three.

Testament and Covenant

The reading of the Bible is needlessly complicated by our unconscious assumption that the words we use today always meant what we understand them to mean. This is simply not so. A good example is the word "testament." Today the word "testament" means a last will, as in "a last will and testament," which becomes effective with the testator's death. Such a meaning is foreign to biblical thought. The Old and New "Testaments" are not wills drawn up by God who is eternal and immortal, but rather refer to sections of the Bible which witness to God's magnificent plan for man's salvation. "Testament" comes from the Latin word *testis*, or "witness." Throughout Old Testament times, inheritance was a matter regulated by custom; a dying person was not free to dispose of the family property at will; it had to remain in the clan or family (Gn 21:10; Dt 21:15-17; Nm 27:8-11; Tb 8:21).

Underlying our word "testament" is the Hebrew word *berith*, or "covenant." It refers to an agreement arrived at, and ritually sealed, between two people. When an agreement had been reached, it was ratified. One of the ways of doing this was to slaughter, then divide an animal in two; the pieces were arranged on the ground and the two persons involved walked between them. This ritual graphically signified the parties' willingness to suffer a similar fate if they did not carry out their part of the bargain (read Gn 15:7-20; Jer 31:31; 34:18-22). The Jews did not simply make a bargain; they would *karath berith*, or "cut a covenant."

Thus one might refer to the two main divisions of the Bible as the Old and the New Covenants. However, again we must understand the term properly to avoid confusion. The English word "covenant" is of Latin origin (*con* + *venire*, a coming-together), and suggests the working out of a compromise between equals. It resembles our word "contract" and is quite misleading. God does not have to negotiate with his creatures. (However, read the charming story of the "bargaining" between Abraham and God in Gn 18:16-33.) The relationship between God and man is not one of equals, but of creator and creature. Contracts in our understanding of the word can be enforced in courts of law; they have teeth, and are hard to break, and deal strictly with facts, not with feeling.

In God's dealings with his Chosen People, his personal concern for man, his generous, loving, merciful nature—in a word, his "feelings"—are everywhere evident. The covenants he makes with man are marvelously interwoven with breathtaking promises. When he made his covenant with Noah, he promised never again to cause a Flood to cover the earth (Gn 9:11). In covenanting with Abraham, he promised a progeny more numerous than the stars (15:5). At Sinai, through Moses, God promised that "you (Israel) of all the nations shall be my very own" (Ex 19:5). The Lord carried out his promises, for he was faithful to his word. The covenant was renewed many times (Jos 24:16-25; 2 Sm 7:8-16; 2 Kgs 23; Neh 8:1-12), and at one point (Jer 31:31-33) he made a promise that surpassed all the others:

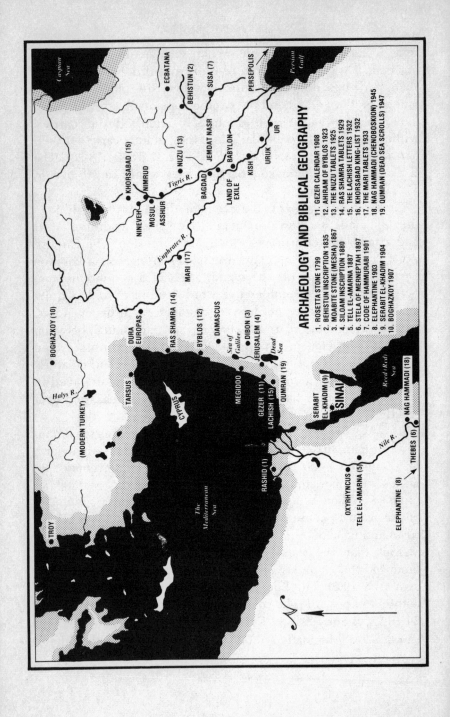

ARCHAEOLOGY AND BIBLICAL GEOGRAPHY

1. ROSETTA STONE 1799
2. BEHISTUN INSCRIPTION 1835
3. MOABITE STONE (MESHA) 1867
4. SILOAM INSCRIPTION 1880
5. TELL EL-AMARNA 1887
6. STELA OF MERNEPTAH 1897
7. CODE OF HAMMURABI 1901
8. ELEPHANTINE 1903
9. SERABIT EL-KHADIM 1904
10. BOGHAZKOY 1907
11. GEZER CALENDAR 1908
12. AHIRAM OF BYBLOS 1923
13. THE NUZU TABLETS 1925
14. RAS SHAMRA TABLETS 1929
15. THE LACHISH LETTERS 1932
16. KHORSABAD KING-LIST 1932
17. THE MARI TABLETS 1933
18. NAG HAMMADI (CHENOBOSKION) 1945
19. QUMRAN (DEAD SEA SCROLLS) 1947

"I will make a *new covenant* . . . ," one written on the heart, not on stone tablets. Our term "New Testament" (or "New Covenant") comes from this text. At the Last Supper, Jesus spoke of his death in these terms (Mk 14:22-25); Paul too sees Christ's death as sealing the New Covenant (1 Cor 11:23-25).

We have learned much about the ancient understanding of the meaning of covenant from an extra-biblical source: the Hittite library discovered at Boghazkoy, a town in modern Turkey (see pp. 176-177). Here there came to light thousands of clay tablets which disclosed the existence, in the second millenium B.C., of two types of international treaties. One resembled our modern contract; it was a "deal" worked out between equals, a parity covenant. The other type, called a suzerainty covenant, was made between a superior and an inferior, between a powerful lord and his vassals. The superior imposed his terms upon the inferior while assuring him protection and security. The vassal's obedience would then flow from his gratitude for what was promised him and done for him.

With this discovery, it is easier to grasp something of the meaning of the word "covenant" used in the Bible. It describes a personal relationship initiated by God with man, involving a pledge or commitment on God's part (and willing loyalty on man's) to the well-being of the people whom he had chosen for his own.

Thus the word "covenant," which is much more descriptive than "testament," is basic to an understanding of the Old Testament. It was also a promise that would be fulfilled in an astounding way by the blood of Jesus. The hopes and ideals of the Old Testament simply melt into the grandeur of such a conception.

Geography

Before starting on our odyssey, we should locate the Bible in space and time. Chronology and geography are the eyes of history, and give us perspective as well as precision. They help

IMPORTANT BIBLICAL DATES
AND
PERTINENT BIBLICAL REFERENCES

(Many dates are approximate)

	The Beginning, or Primeval History	Gn 1-11
BC 1850-	**The Patriarchal Period** Abraham	Gn 12-50
1250-	**Moses and Joshua**	Ex Nm Dt Jos Lv
1200-931	**From the Judges to Solomon** David 1010-970 Solomon 970-931— The Golden Age	Jgs; 1-2 Sm; 1 Kgs 1-11; 1 Chr; 2 Chr 1-9
931-721	**The Divided Kingdom** The Fall of Samaria 721	1 Kgs 12-22; 2 Kgs 1-17; 2 Chr 10-28; Am Ho Is Mi
721-587	**The End of the Kingdom of Judah** The Exile 587-538	2 Kgs 18-25; 2 Chr 29-36; Zep Na Hb Jer Ez
587-333	**The Persian Period** Return from the Exile 538	Ezr Neh Hg Zec Mal Jb Prv Sg Ru Pss Jl Ob
333-63	**The Hellenistic Period** The Maccabees: 168-37	1-2 Mc Dn Jon Tb
63 BC-135 AD	**The Roman Period**	
BC 6-8	The Birth of Jesus Christ	Mt Lk
AD 30	Death of Jesus	Mt Mk Lk Jn
45-58	The Missionary Journeys of St. Paul	Acts, Letters
50-99	The NT is Written First Jewish Revolt 66-70 AD Second Jewish Revolt 132-135	

establish fixed points of reference, so that, instead of marching Abraham and his descendants to and from some imaginary Shangri-la, we will know where he and they belong in history, and on the map.

Abraham came from Ur of the Chaldees (Gn 11:28), and his sons for a time lived in Egypt. If we draw a line between those two countries along the rivers, it will describe a crescent—the Fertile Crescent, as it has been called. These are the lands of the Bible. They extend from the Persian Gulf up along the Tigris and the Euphrates (the territory between the rivers was called Mesopotamia, which simply means "between the rivers"), across and down Syria and Palestine, and into Egypt and the Nile.

The Bible has roots and branches in many lands, and throughout history the Israelites rubbed elbows with many other peoples whose names often crop up in the Bible. The Chaldeans, called Babylonians after the seventh century B.C., are mentioned, but the Sumerians, who lived in the same general area of southeast Babylonia, are not. This despite the fact that the Sumerians were a brilliant people whose writings and culture exercised a considerable influence upon Israel. The Phoenicians were peoples who lived to the north of Palestine. The whole area stretching from Syria through Palestine was at one time called Canaan; its inhabitants were Canaanites. All these people are lumped together as Semites (the term is of philological invention). The Semitic peoples are the descendants of Noah's son Shem, according to the Table of Nations given in Genesis 10. They are the Elamites, Assyrians, Aramaeans, and the ancestors of the Hebrews. Actually the principle of such groupings is not so much of racial affinity as it is of historical and geographical relationship.

To the south and west of the Promised Land lay Egypt, already ancient when Abraham began his journey to the land which the Lord would show him. The Egyptians are described as descendants of Ham, another of Noah's sons (Gn 10:6). Again, the grouping of his descendants is not ethnographic, but is the

CHRONOLOGY FROM THE SCHISM TO THE EXILE

KINGS OF JUDAH		KINGS OF ISRAEL		PROPHETS
Rehoboam	931-913	Jeroboam I	931-910	
Abijah	913-911			
Asa	911-870	Nadab	910-909	
		Baasha	909-886	
		Elah	886-885	
		Zimri	885	
		Omri	885-874	
		Ahab	874-853	
Jehoshaphat	870-848			
Jehoram	848-841	Ahaziah	853-852	
Ahaziah	841	Jehoram	852-841	
Athaliah	841-835	Jehu	841-814	
Joash	835-796	Jehoahaz	814-798	
		Joash	798-783	
Amaziah	796-781			Amos
Uzziah	781-740	Jeroboam II	783-743	Hosea
		Zechariah	743	Isaiah
		Shallum	743	Micah
		Menahem	743-738	
Jotham	740-736	Pekahiah	738-737	
		Pekah	737-732	
Ahaz	736-716	Hoshea	732-724	
		FALL OF SAMARIA	721	
Hezekiah	716-687			
Manasseh	687-642			
Amon	642-640			Zephaniah
Josiah	640-609	FALL OF NINEVEH	612	Jeremiah
Jehoahaz	609			Baruch
Jehoiakim	609-598			Nahum
Jehoiakin	598			Habakkuk
Zedekiah	598-587			Ezekiel
FALL OF JERUSALEM	587			
Deportation	587			
THE EXILE	587-538	FALL OF BABYLON	538	
				Haggai
				Zechariah
				Malachi
				Joel
				Obadiah
				Jonah
				Daniel

result of historical and geographic factors.

Between Egypt and Assyria-Babylon existed an ancient and a bitter rivalry. Many wars were fought between these two lands and Israel—caught in the middle—was a battleground. Israel's own brief periods of prosperity and glory coincided with times when the great powers were weak, or too preoccupied with domestic affairs to worry about their far-flung empires.

It is surely one of the ironies of history that the Promised Land should for so many centuries have borne the name of Palestine, which comes from the name of Israel's ancient enemy, the Philistines.

The Bible and Time

Genesis 1-11:26 belongs to a time that we might call Proto or Primeval or even Pre-History. For it, no chronology exists. Bible history, as we understand history, begins with Abraham. A date of about 1850 B.C. can be assigned to Abraham. He and his story fit in rather well with what we know of that period. But then some 600 years elapse, bringing us to Moses and the Exodus; many accept a date ca. 1250 B.C. for Moses and the Exodus from Egypt. The first independently verified biblical date is that of David, ca. 1010 B.C.* After Solomon's reign (970-931), there ensued the great Schism which inaugurated the Divided Kingdom. Some 200 years later, Samaria, the capital of Israel, was captured by the Assyrian Sargon II, and a mass deportation followed. Jerusalem, left now without a buffer to the north, was doomed. It fell to the Babylonian monarch, Nebuchadrezzar, in 587 B.C. The date marks the beginning of the Babylonian Exile, which lasted for almost fifty years. When Cyrus the Persian became master of Babylon in 538 B.C., one of his first acts was to allow the captive Jews to return to their homeland. The Great Return was viewed almost as a second Exodus (Is 40). However, after the Persians, the Greeks under

---

*Pharaoh Shishak (935-914 B.C.) of the 22nd Dynasty sacked Jerusalem in 918, in the fifth year of Jeroboam, Solomon's successor. Working back from this gives us a date ca. 1000 for David (1 Kgs 14:25).

Alexander (d. 323) captured the land. In 64 B.C., the Romans took a firm hold on Syria, and from then on were the dominant force in the Mid-East. Twice the Jews revolted against Roman rule; the first effort climaxed in the siege and fall of Jerusalem to Titus between 66-70 A.D.; the second was ruthlessly put down by Hadrian (132-135 A.D.). Under him, Jerusalem, rebuilt along Roman lines, became Aelia Capitolina, and a long darkness settled upon Judea.

All this has only set the stage for our journey through the Bible. This is a journey all of us should take, for it will bring the reader to the God who awaits him at its end, and who is with him every step of the way.

TWO

THE BIBLE IS WRITTEN

Portions of the Bible are among the oldest of man's written documents. They date from an era when ancient man was beginning to put his oral histories into written form. All of the Bible was written in forms, languages, and styles that modern men find unfamiliar. By learning something about how writing evolved, we can appreciate the ingenuity and inventiveness of our forebears, and something about the nature of the Bible as well.

Man first began to write in Mesopotamia about 5000 years ago. Once he had learned this skill, no surface was safe from him. Man has pounded or scratched his name and thoughts into stone, metal, wood, and plaster; he has painted them on cloth, leaves, and rocks. Graffiti are as old as man-who-could-write. Of all these materials, however, clay was the one used most extensively. The land between the Tigris and the Euphrates Rivers provided a good clean clay upon which were impressed business transactions, legends, and religious epics. The clay was inexpensive, and, when oven-baked, clay tablets became practically indestructible. Many thousands of such tablets, recovered from the ruins of ancient cities, and now distributed among scholars and museums all over the world, patiently await their turn to tell their story. Along with the tablets are a good number of shards, or bits of broken pottery with writing upon them. These are called *ostraca* (see p. 168).

At the other end of the Fertile Crescent, Egyptian scribes cut or painted their hieroglyphics on pillars, statues, walls of tombs, and on papyrus. Egypt is the home of papyrus, the fragile writing material which has—although less successfully than clay tablets—survived the corrosive hand of time. It allows us a glimpse into the secular and religious world of the Pharaohs and their people.

We shall look briefly at the way writing has evolved. Then we shall examine ancient writing materials, biblical and non-biblical styles of writing, shapes and sizes of the Bible, and the creation of chapters and verses. After these considerations, we can venture to describe the "birth of the Bible."

The Evolution of Writing

The earliest evidence of man's creative ability are cave drawings, primitive tools, and intelligent markings upon durable materials like stone, clay, and metal. Some of these early artifacts were cylinder seals—small incised bits of stone about the size of a small piece of chalk, pierced through from end to end and worn around the owner's neck. When the seal was rolled over soft clay, it left an impression—a hunting or religious scene, or the owner's "mark." Each seal was a unique work of art. The seals are of great antiquity, showing up at Uruk on the lower Euphrates during the fourth millenium B.C. Pictures of these "messages" can be admired in Pritchard's *The Ancient Near East in Pictures*.

Eventually, after many hundreds of years, ancient man hit upon a more flexible way of communication, the *pictograph*. This was a series of miniature, simplified drawings of, say, a house, a deer, a dog, a spear, a hand or foot. Strung together, they told a visual story, such as the story of a hunt. Pictographs first appeared at Kish, not far from Uruk, ca. 3500 B.C. However, the pictograph was severely limited, and after another long period there came into being the *ideograph*, or *ideogram*. By 2900 B.C. at Jemdat Nasr (also on the lower Euphrates), the pictographs had become more abstract or stylized. Each sign represented a single word, but—and this was the advance—that sign could be used also as part of another word. To give an English example, the symbols for *eye* and *land* could be put together to form the word *island*. By associating definite sounds to the ideograms, writing became syllabic. Nebuchadrezzar was written Ne-bu-cha-drez-zar, and the individual syllables could be used in a variety of ways. Ancient syllabaries have been discovered, the equivalent of our old spelling books.

The decisive breakthrough in the art of written communication came with the separation of consonants from vowels, and the development of *alphabetic writing*. Probably Indo-European in origin, the first alphabet dates to about 2000 B.C., and the first extant example of its use is the inscription around the sarcophagus cover of Ahiram of Byblos.

We mention briefly here the languages of two great empires whose destinies were intertwined with that of Israel. Assyria lay to the northeast, Egypt to the southwest. In both languages one looks vainly for any reference, however brief, to the Hebrews, thus to be able to date and locate and understand better some of the events mentioned in the Bible.

The Hebrew language belongs to a group of northwest Semitic languages which includes Moabite, Phoenician, and Ugaritic. (See chart p. 149.) It is not known whether Abraham could write or read, but Moses, educated at an Egyptian court, could and did, as the Bible attests.

During their many years in Egypt, the Israelites doubtless many times looked upon that fascinating style of writing which is called *hieroglyphic*. The word comes from the Greek *hieros* or "sacred," and *glypho* which means "carving." Egyptian scribes were skillful men with an eye for beauty, and their hieroglyphs, incised into pillars or painted on the walls of tombs, never cease to intrigue the visitor to Egypt. Used for over 3000 years, hieroglyphic writing (which was both pictorial and phonetic), became *hieratic*, a cursive form, and *demotic*, a more abbreviated form. The last known use of hierogly-

phics was in a religious inscription found on the island of
Philae (394 A.D.).

The second intriguing form of writing, familiar to almost
everybody who has visited a good museum or leafed through
the pages of the *National Geographic,* is called *cuneiform.* This
is a wedge-shaped kind of writing (*cuneus* in Latin means
"wedge"). Around 3000 B.C., Sumerian scribes began to use a
reed stylus, triangular in shape at one end, to make impressions
on wet clay, a material that discouraged circular or curved lines.
The oldest cuneiform texts were pictographic, but the forms
soon became idealized, and then syllabic. This remarkable language, once the official language of an empire stretching from
the Caucasus to the Indian Ocean, and from the Indus River to
the Mediterranean, was deciphered through the discovery of
the Behistun Inscription (see p. 170).

Biblical Styles of Writing

The famous saint with a short fuse, St. Jerome, translator of
the Vulgate, seems to have coined the word *uncial* to describe
the style of writing found in the oldest and most important
Greek and Latin manuscripts of the Bible.* Incensed at the roar
of criticism which his careful corrections of the gospel texts had
touched off, Jerome struck back:

> If I have undertaken to replace omissions, correct mistakes,
> and set forth the Church's mysteries in pure, reliable lan-
> guage, should I be censured by picky, malicious readers? Let
> them stay with their old texts, written though they be on pur-
> ple parchments in letters of silver and gold, or even in what
> they call uncial letters.

Obviously, Jerome preferred a good text badly written on poor
materials to a "corrupt" text beautifully lettered on expensive

---

*Nothing need be said here about Hebrew or Aramaic writing (see Chapter
Eight). The term *uncial* applies to Greek and Latin manuscripts.

parchment. But it is his use of the word *uncial* here that chiefly interests us. The word may come from the Latin word for "thumbnail." Uncial letters were like our capitals; each large letter *(majuscule)* had to be written separately. A more rapid or cursive script developed in time and was used on parchment. Papyrus was too rough for speedy writing.

For purely economic reasons, no room was wasted on expensive parchment. Space between words was eliminated. The beginning of St. John's Gospel in Greek looked something like this: ENAPXHHNOΛC, and in Latin like this: INPRINCIPIO-ERATVERBUM. Abbreviations were very common, and one might encounter lines like John 1:14: ETVERBŪCARO-FACTŪEST or even (2:4) NODVEIT, where the bars over the letters stood for M's or N's, thus: *Et Verbum Caro Factum Est,* and *Nondum venit.* The divine name was frequently abbreviated as ΘC (theos) IC and XC (Jesous, Christos).

The early part of the ninth century A.D. witnessed a revolution in writing with the introduction of the *minuscule,* or smaller letter. These letters, written with a running or cursive hand, took up less space and the scribe did not have to lift the pen after each letter. The gain was considerable, but it was purchased at the expense of beauty.

Sentences were first punctuated sometime during the sixth and seventh centuries, but it was not until the eleventh century that words were written separately, or spaced apart. Accents and breathing marks were introduced into Greek manuscripts. The punctuation can be of crucial importance. The UBS *Greek New Testament* (1976) notes 600 places where the punctuation makes a difference in the sense of a passage.

Writing Materials

Most of the writing in the ancient world was done on papyrus, a kind of paper made from a reed that grew in the delta of the Nile and also in parts of Italy. The plant reached a height of twelve to fifteen feet, and was used to make baskets (Ex 2:3) and even boats (Is 18:2). Used for writing toward the end of the fourth millenium B.C., it was later introduced into Syria and Palestine. Papyrus was last used in the seventh century A.D.

In his famous *National History,* the Roman historian Pliny described how papyrus was made into writing material. The core of the plant, as thick as a man's wrist, was sliced into thin vertical sections which were then placed side by side on a flat surface. Other strips were laid over these at right angles. The whole was then moistened (Pliny observed that Nile water was the best for this), pressed out, and hung in the sun to dry. Strips about the size of a sheet of our typewriting paper were sewed or pasted together along the short side and then rolled up. Twenty or so sheets would make an average papyrus roll of some thirteen feet; the rolls were about a foot and a half in diameter.

The Harris Papyrus is in a class (and probably a room) all by itself, being 133 feet in length and 11 inches high. The Egyptian *Book of the Dead* was written on rolls ranging from 50 to 100 feet in length. It is interesting to note that our English word "volume" comes from the Latin *volumen,* which means something rolled up.

Being quite fragile and brittle when dry, papyrus rolls were not easy to handle, but that problem was cleverly surmounted. Two rods with a knob or ball at one end were attached along both ends of a written scroll. When a reader wished to read, he would simply fit the two knobs on the top of the sticks into fixed, y-shaped uprights, pull the sticks out at the bottom to a forty-five degree angle, and untwist the roll (while rolling it up on the other stick) to the desired place. In modern synagogues, the Law and the Prophets are preserved in scrolls, but are so boxed and hinged that they can be used with little danger of tearing.

In a dry climate, papyrus can last indefinitely. The first papyrus finds came from the charred ruins of Pompeii; miraculously, 150 scrolls survived there, but the most important finds were those made in Egypt. Near Aswan, rain falls perhaps once in twenty years, and throughout the land papyrus has been spared from humidity. In 1778 an antique dealer acquired a roll of papyrus from Egyptian peasants who informed him that such "sticks" gave forth a pleasant odor when burned!* Letters and contracts were written on small sheets of papyrus, which were rolled, tied in the middle, and sealed with clay, upon which one impressed his seal. To open such an ancient scroll without causing it to fly into a thousand pieces remains a delicate problem. First the clay and string have to be removed. Next the "stick" is put under a bell jar and over a saucer of water. In response to the moisture, the papyrus slowly becomes pliable and can be spread out, cleaned, and then sealed between plates of glass. Once this is done, it can be handled and studied at leisure.

The papyrus was prepared by a scribe, a craftsman held in high esteem in Egypt. Scribes were even depicted on some monuments along with the tools of their trade. One of these tools was a writing case containing the scribe's pens and inks (see Ez 9:2-11). The pens were sometimes of metal, but usually were made from a reed; one held the sharpened end of a reed between the teeth, chewed it gently, and produced a tiny paint brush. It was a very distant cousin indeed to the ballpoint pen; closer, perhaps, to our modern fiber-tip pen. Making ink was a more complicated problem. Black ink could be made from soot combined with gum tragacanth. It was usable when moistened with water. Walnut shells and iron produced a black dye. Red ink (with which all ages are familiar, but for different reasons) was made from nutgall, ferrous sulfate, and water.

In Pritchard's monumental *Ancient Near Eastern Texts* (ANET, 431-434) there are two delightful essays awaiting the modern reader. One is "In Praise of Learned Scribes," and the other "A Satire on the Trades," sketching out in detail the importance of the scribe and the wretchedness of those who had to work at nonscribal trades (read Sir 38:24-34).

The grain of papyrus was straight and even. The front—the side with the horizontal grain—was called the *recto;* the other side, where the stripes were vertical, was called the *verso.*

---

*For a more dramatic and sinister burning, read Jer 36:26-32.

(These terms, of course, are Latin, not Egyptian.) The *recto* was preferred for writing, as the grain guided the scribe and helped him keep the letters of the same size. The writing was usually in vertical columns some two or three inches wide, and one opened the scroll from right to left (and definitely *not* from top to bottom, as Hollywood prefers). Incidentally, only the very poor wrote on both sides of a papyrus (or stone slab); such a product was called an *opisthograph*.

Ancient writing was a slow affair. A good scribe could average three syllables per minute, which would make about seventy-two words per hour. This is the ancient equivalent of about six or seven lines of typing! A sheet of papyrus held about 140 words. Thus it took the scribe about two hours to fill an ordinary page! The tiny letter to Philemon, 335 words long, would have taken a scribe more than two hours to write. The letter to the Romans contains 7100 words. It would have required fifty sheets of papyrus and about one hundred hours of actual writing.

It is very interesting to consider the pace of ancient writing, especially in view of the temperament of an explosive character like Paul who had so much to say. Was Paul frequently interrupted by Tertius, one of his scribes, with the complaint "Hold on, Paul! Wait a minute!... Now, what did you say?" Indeed, in Paul's letters, it is sometimes difficult to see the connection of one sentence with another. Did the Apostle sometimes lose his train of thought? That is possible. There was also time pressure. Both Paul and his scribe Tertius worked at a trade—they were tent-makers—and there must have been days when two or three hours of writing were more than they could manage. Perhaps it took them as long as thirty or forty days to write Romans. One never gets the impression that Paul revised his letters. Only the letter to the Hebrews manifests smoothness in style and elegance in expression along with an orderly exposition of thought. For these reasons, most scholars have attributed the actual writing of Hebrews to Tertius, or Apollos, or others, For the rest, the remark of 2 Peter 3:16 is much to the point: "There are certain passages in [Paul's letters] hard to understand."

Some Famous Papyri

The international list of recognized papyri* now runs to eighty-one items. Two, however, are of particular importance, and their discovery caused great excitement in the world of biblical scholarship. The first is the John Rylands Greek Papyrus, first published in 1935 by the Manchester University Press. It is the oldest known bit of New Testament writing, dating possibly to 94, and no later than 125-135 A.D. A tiny fragment (3.5 by 2.3 inches), it contains recognizable scraps of four verses of John's Gospel: chapter 18, verses 31-32 and 37-38. The fragment was once part of a book, and is clear evidence that the Fourth Gospel was in circulation in Egypt at a very early date. The texts involved contain Pilate's questions: "Are you the king of the Jews?" and "Truth! What is that?"

In 1966, Martin Bodmer, founder of the Library of World Literature, published a papyrus which now bears his name, the Papyrus Bodmer II. It is 6.4 by 5.6 inches in size, and it is seventy-five pages long. The text, once again, is that of John. A few pages have been lost, and the section on the woman taken in adultery (Jn 7:54-8:11) is missing. It is written in a good clear uncial hand and belongs to a date ca. 200 A.D. Some assign an even earlier date to it (ca. 150 A.D.).

The proximity of these two papyri to the apostolic age (according to tradition John died ca. 99 A.D.) lends them a special value, for they represent a text of the Fourth Gospel that is less than a hundred years old. When these papyri are compared to the later parchment texts of that gospel, it is clear that they are substantially identical. This is reassuring, for some have feared that John's original gospel was not the same text that emerged several hundred years later in our oldest Greek manuscripts. The Rylands and Bodmer papyri indicate a remarkable fidelity in the transmission of the apostolic text.

---

*The only ancient Hebrew manuscript known before 1947 was the Nash Papyrus (ca. 150 B.C.), which contains the Ten Commandments and Dt 6:1. (See below, Chapter Nine.)

During the nineteenth and early twentieth centuries it was sometimes argued that the Fourth Gospel was the product, not of apostolic times, but of a much later period. The reason for saying this was a preconception that the writer of the Fourth Gospel drew his themes of light and darkness, truth and spirit, good and evil, etc., from Gnostic literature, which could not have been current at the close of the first century. This view has now been abandoned as papyrus evidence to the contrary builds up.

For the reader who is curious to know how scholars work with papyri, which are often fragmentary pieces like a jigsaw puzzle, there is now available an excellent work, *Encountering New Testament Manuscripts*, by Jack Finegan. It contains pictures, transcriptions of the texts, and discussions about papyri and other ancient manuscripts written on parchment. Finegan has treated the same material in a more general way in his *Light From the Ancient Past*, a readable synthesis of Near Eastern archaeology's contribution to the study of the Bible; it likewise features many photographs of manuscripts, ancient artifacts, and excavations of ancient sites.

Parchment

Leather coexisted with papyrus as a writing material. The skins of animals were used for writing purposes as early as the seventeenth century B.C. In time, the process of preparing the leather was refined, and parchment came into being. How this happened is recorded in a probably apocryphal story related by two Roman historians, Varro and Pliny. The story incidentally illustrates how little human nature has changed.

It seems that Eumenes II (197-169 B.C.), king of Pergamum, a city on the west coast of what is now Turkey (and not far from ancient Troy) was seized by a royal ambition to assemble a library that would equal, if not surpass, the famous library in Alexandria in Egypt. Upon hearing of Eumenes' project, King Ptolemy V Epiphanes (203-181 B.C.) of Egypt promptly imposed an embargo on the export of papyrus! Eumenes' setback was only temporary, however, for the story goes on to say that, necessity proving once more to be the mother of invention, another type of writing material was developed and was named after the city of its birth: parchment, or *membrana pergamena*.

Parchment was made from skins of animals. The hides were first soaked in limewater, then scraped, stretched, and dried. Next they were rubbed smooth with chalk or pumice. The result was a kind of writing material that could be handled freely, and could be used on both sides; it was more durable than papyrus but also heavier and shinier. Ink was applied to the skin with reed or metal pens. (*Vellum* is simply parchment made from the skins of young animals.)

The use of papyrus for writing continued on until well into the fourth century A.D. Parchment, the new material, was not without its defects, of course. It creased, crumpled up or wrinkled, and in time it too wore out. But it was better than papyrus, and when the Talmud (see Chapter Eight) came to be written down, perhaps not until well after the time of Christ, it prescribed that the Law was to be written on parchment scrolls. The Talmud further prescribed that worn-out copies of the Law could not be destroyed, no doubt out of respect for the sacred name therein, but were to be retired to a *geniza,* a chest or cupboard located in or close to a synagogue. The most famous geniza is the one discovered by Abraham Firkowitz (d. 1874) in a medieval synagogue in the old quarter of Cairo, Egypt. The collection he found contained not less than 1582 manuscripts, none of them older than the tenth century A.D. Thus once again, we see that the value of the papyri lies in their great antiquity.

The Forms of the Bible

It appears strange to us that the ancient scroll or roll form persisted for so long. The first books, written on papyrus and leather, were scrolls, resembling a modern roll of paper towels. They were unwieldy, and to find a particular passage, one had to unroll them foot by foot. Eventually the scroll form was replaced by the *codex*. The word comes from the Latin *caudex*, meaning the trunk of a tree. In this connection it refers to thin, shingle-type leaves of wood which formed a book when bound together along one side. Once the thin, wax-coated wood was replaced by parchment, the book became a practical, usable, efficient form, and well within a hundred years had clearly established its superiority. From the late first century on, the book form steadily gained in popularity.

We are interested in such developments because we are interested in the Bible. Our earliest manuscripts of the Bible are called codices, and they are all in book form. As has been already mentioned, the text of these codices was continuous, without spaces between words. However, marginal signs indicated the beginnings of new sections. It was not until 1226 that Stephen Langton, a professor at the University of Paris and later archbishop of Canterbury, divided the text of the Bible into chapters. What he did was to combine a number of sections or pericopes into single consecutive chapters, and did a remarkably good job of it. Only here and there did he make a mistake: Philippians 4:1 should certainly be the last verse of the preceding chapter, and 1 Corinthians 11:1 belongs after 10:33.

Another notable textual improvement occurred in the year 1551 when the famous printer, Robert Stephen, also known as Estienne or Stephanus, introduced into the Bible the numbering of verses worked out in 1528 by Santes Pagnini. Some of Stephen's contemporaries looked upon the innovation as an act of irreverence, but, as the utility of the system became evident, the opposition disappeared. Verse numbering is now universally accepted in all Bibles. In recent years the numbers have been reduced in size and made as inconspicuous as possible; they have been put in the inner margin (in the Jerusalem Bible), the outer margin (in the New English Bible) and back into the text (in the New American Bible). But in any arrangement, it is now mere child's play to pinpoint any sentence anywhere in the Bible.

From the beginning, believers selected suitable passages from the gospels and elsewhere for use in religious assemblies. These sections go by the name of *pericopes,* a Greek word which means passages that can be "cut out" or can stand by themselves. When such passages are brought together they make up a *lectionary.*

With this basically descriptive information now before us, it is time to turn to the processes that actually produced the Bible.

The Birth of the Bible

Why do people write books? Some mysterious chemistry in the blood, a fever in the brain? Some write to make money, some because they want to say something that needs saying. Others write to share knowledge or to entertain. Some books reveal an author's towering indignation, some justify existing situations, others preserve a history in writing. "Of the writing of books, there is no end."

Christians believe that some men have written books because God wanted them to, and gently managed to get them to do it. We wonder at the value of some of what they have written (for example, Gn 10; Jos 13-21), but apparently God desired a record kept of such things, along with what he had done, and what hopes he entertains for man. His promises, goodness, and love are all spelled out in his book—the Bible. He *is* its author.

God's "book" did not fall from heaven ready-made. It came into being slowly, across many centuries. Reflecting upon what had happened throughout history, the reflective Israelite began to perceive God-at-work, particularly in crucial moments in the life of the Chosen People such as the Exodus, and later in the Exile and Return. Read aloud, the early stories of the Old Testament transport one back to flickering campfires in the desert, where God and the patriarchs met and conversed. The stories sound just right; they are faithful echoes of a tenacious oral tradition which was later given permanency in writing. Many such traditions existed, scattered about as so many bits of a mosaic in the memories of Israelite tribes to the north and south. The content of these traditions varied according to the interests of their makers. In the course of 2000 years, some of these sources long ago ceased to exist. We know this from the casual references made to them in the Bible: there was the *Book of the Just* (Jos 10:13); the *Book of the Annals of the Kings of Judah* [and] ... *of Israel* (1 Kgs 15:6; 16:5, *passim*), and the *Memoirs of Nehemiah* (2 Mc 2:13). They have disappeared. The same is true of the New Testament: part of the Corinthian correspondence, a letter to the Laodiceans (Col 4:16), and other sources have been lost. The assumption that God always sees to the preservation of works he has motivated is historically without foundation. (For a discussion, see *The Jerome Biblical Commentary*, 67:54.) Sources can vanish like people, once they have performed the role assigned them.

The Role of the Scribe

As the writings which we now know as the Old Testament came together, the scribes of the ancient royal courts of Israel played a central role. Ancient writings were generally associated with the royal courts, where there was both money and the motive to write. Among the impulses that drove ancient man to write were pride and self-justification. One reads of the wickedness of the defeated foe and of how the gods and the people favored the victorious king. One can detect a political flavor in this; writing was a bit of propaganda justifying the royal family, showing the line of descent which led to the reigning king, with his splendid palace, armies, and yes, his taxes.

The Bible three times lists the men who assisted David and Solomon in the administration of the land. Among these men, the scribe was singled out. He was probably the king's private secretary and the secretary of state as well. Clearly a man of power and influence, the scribe had to be conversant with matters discussed at the highest levels. He had to be a man of shrewd judgment, and familiar with the royal archives. It is likely that in the cultural explosion that started under the poet-king David and flourished under Solomon, the royal scribe was deeply involved. For it is probable that at this early date a major effort was made to gather materials and to bring together in permanent written form the laws and traditions that molded the people. In this the scribe must have played a central role.

Eventually David and Solomon themselves became part of that tradition. It is safe to assume that by the time of the Exile in 587 B.C. there were already in existence bodies of writings which contained the historical and juridical traditions of the people. Added to these were the far-reaching reform measures of Hezekiah (2 Kgs 18:1-8), and later of Josiah (2 Kgs 22), copies of which were deposited in the Temple. (A similar practice is known to have happened elsewhere in the Middle East. The Code of Hammurabi was set up in the temple at Sippar.)

However, at this point, writing had not assumed the importance it now enjoys. Far more important was memory. It has been amply documented that the human memory is capable of astonishing feats, especially when there is hardly any other means of safeguarding precious information. Even today, when we largely rely on "written memory," there are people who are gifted with extraordinary memories, who have "total recall." This is not a new phenomenon. When Jerusalem fell in 587 B.C., the scribes who had the moral patrimony of the nation accurately stored away in memory were among those sought out for immediate deportation. Their material world may have lain behind them in ruins, but they carried their real treasure with them in their heads.

From the crucible of the Babylonian Exile came something precious: a retelling, a reshaping, a reinterpretation of all the nation's history and laws and wisdom. The historical sagas and stories were put into some sort of chronological order; juridical material was brought up to date; and the wisdom books were given shape. The process of shaping what we know as the Old Testament continued after the Return, but the major work was done especially in the period of the Exile.

The Law

The core of the Old Testament is the Law—Genesis, Exodus, Leviticus, Numbers, and Deuteronomy—the first five books of the Bible, also known as the Pentateuch. These books recount the creation of man, the early history of the Hebrew people, their deliverance from Egypt, and settlement in Canaan. The Pentateuch also contains the laws which God enjoined on the Hebrews after he made a covenant with them.

For almost 2000 years, Moses has been called the author of these first five books of the Bible. However, with the birth of critical historical methods of biblical study in the last century, this position can no longer be maintained, or, at least, must be modified. The books in question contain such a wide variety of styles, diverse interests, and so much repetition and unevenness, that a unity of authorship seems quite out of the question.

To explain the facts as they were known a century ago, the Documentary Theory was formulated. According to this view, the Pentateuch is made up of four strands of tradition which emanated from different times and places. It was argued that all of these documents were late compositions, written in the fifth century B.C., long after Moses. Such in brief was the theory of Graf, developed brilliantly by the German scholar Julius Wellhausen. This theory enjoyed a great vogue and dominated Old Testament thinking for several decades, but eventually a reaction set in. More realistically, it was seen that Moses could have and did use sources, many of them of extreme antiquity. Many Pentateuchal laws and institutions are now known to have had extra-biblical counterparts far back in time, an important bit of information that Wellhausen did not have when he developed his theory.

Scholars today therefore prefer to speak of the materials in the Pentateuch not as sources or documents, but as *traditions*. These traditions were long influential in different times and places. For example, they would be recited in temples or holy places. Finally, the various traditions were brought together under the influence of some powerful personality into something close to the form we have them now. Let us see if we can observe the process at work.

First of all, there is the *Yahwistic tradition* (J), so named because of its consistent use of Yahweh as the divine name. Its language is pictorial and graphic. It is also anthropomorphic: it describes God with human qualities. God molds clay into a man, into whom he then breathes life; he brings the animals to Adam, builds up one of Adam's ribs into a woman. The Yahwistic tradition presents God almost as one would present a human being, but, along with the lively tone, it also provides profound answers to man's most perplexing problems.

The *Elohistic tradition* (E) features a stately style. God is consistently called *Elohim* (the common name for God). In it a good distance is maintained between God and man, but it also voices things of astonishing theological depth. It is believed that this tradition, in contrast to that of J, originated in the northern kingdom of Israel.

In the Yahwistic and Elohistic traditions there is relatively little legislation, but in a third and *Priestly tradition* (P) there is little else. The Law is everything. The sanctuary, its feasts, sacrifices, and vestments are given full attention, as are the genealogies. The authors seem to have been fascinated with numbers as well.

These three traditions (J, E, P) appear throughout Genesis, Exodus, Leviticus, and Numbers, but the fifth and last book of the Pentateuch represents an independent tradition, the *Deuteronomic* (D). It was written from a different viewpoint. Its Deuteronomic Code (12-26 and 28) is framed by Moses' eloquent discourses with their constantly repeated theme that God is not lofty and distant, but loving. He chose Israel to be his people. "What great nation is there that has gods so close to it as the Lord, our God, is to us whenever we call upon him?" (Dt 4:7).

Tradition was not wrong in seeing the importance of Moses in forming the Pentateuch. He was the force which brought all the traditions together, even those passages which clearly are post-

Mosaic. Moses was the great lawgiver and leader, a unifying force; when changes were made in response to new situations, or new laws were added for the same reason, care was taken to see that it was all done *according to the mind of Moses*. Without this, there would have been no Old Testament.

Only a very naive person would picture Moses as a "scissors and paste" writer who only had to piece together what others had written. He certainly made use of sources older than himself, but he made unique contributions to the finished product, such as his personal experiences with the Lord. The actual literary form of the Pentateuch is less important than the fact that what we read in the first five books traces back to the extraordinary figure of Moses.

The Bible does not end with Moses (ca. 1250 B.C.). Another thousand years of formation lay ahead of the Old Testament and it is not always easy to follow its development, but much can be guessed from the mere shape of the end product.

After Moses, two other strains of thought developed in Israel which were ultimately joined to his legislation and to early history. The first of these additions was embodied in what we call sapiential or wisdom literature; the second, in the prophets.

Wisdom Literature

The acquisition of wisdom is a very ancient and honorable pursuit, as the literature of Mesopotamia, Egypt, and other cultures attests. Inevitably, man's thoughts focus on the mystery and meaning of life and of suffering, on what is wise and what is foolish behavior. These reflections are expressed in proverbs, maxims, fables, and poetry; some of the more felicitous of these circulated freely throughout the Fertile Crescent. The story of a Babylonian Job, for example, was widely known, and the "Wisdom of Ahiqar" was very popular, appearing in many languages. Canaanite wise men and sages from northern Arabia contributed to the wisdom literature as well. Egypt might almost be considered its home; the "Instruction of Amen-em-opet" was admired far beyond Egypt. However, only in Israel, where the pursuit of wisdom began under Solomon in the tenth century B.C., was a successful attempt made to transcend the purely mundane considerations of life and its meaning. In Israel alone, wisdom became spiritualized, going far beyond the usual pragmatic advice about how to win friends and influence people. Wisdom, in fact, was associated with God himself in many passages (Prv 8:22-31). The Old Testament teaching on wisdom reached its climax in Wisdom 7:22-8:1, where wisdom is described as a person endowed with exclusively divine attributes: omnipotence, holiness, and changelessness. In such passages, Christian tradition has with insight discerned glimmerings of what would in time become the doctrine of the Trinity. Thus the Old Testament concept of wisdom is religious, and is well summed up in the oft-quoted "The beginning of wisdom is the fear of the Lord" (Prv 1:7).

In our Bibles there are five specifically wisdom books: Job, Proverbs, Qoheleth, Sirach, and Wisdom. To these were added the Song of Songs (which is hardly suited to the genre) and the Psalms. Characteristic of this genre is its poetic form. Here we must learn a rule: "Parallelism is the great law of Hebrew poetry." This requires some explanation, and it will be time well spent, inasmuch as poetic forms appear throughout the Old Testament, and even in the New Testament.

Parallelism in the Wisdom Literature

In poetry, one may choose his own form, so to speak: so many feet (or beats) to a line, lines rhymed or unrhymed. This example from Shakespeare's "The Rape of Lucrece" illustrates both rhyme and precise meter.

What win I if I gain the thing I seek
   A dream, a breath, a froth of fleeting joy;
Who buys a moment's mirth to wail a week,
   Or sells eternity to gain a toy?

Each line contains exactly ten syllables; every other line rhymes: seek ... week; joy ... toy, to the pleasure of the ear and the delight of the mind. In poetry there is an almost endless variety. Some poems have only two lines, some four, or eight, or fourteen or more, and the number of syllables to a line varies greatly. In classic English poetry, there is almost always rhyme.

By contrast, Hebrew poetry never employed rhyme, but is governed instead by the laws of parallelism. This means that Hebrew poetry matches ideas instead of words. The ideas are matched and balanced, set off one against the other: half-line against half-line; verse against verse; or groups of verses against other groups of verses. Once the reader has begun to notice this pattern he will begin to appreciate the artistry involved. Parallelism is extremely ingenious, and is no doubt more difficult to work out in practice than to describe after the fact.

Three different types of parallelism are employed in the psalms and wisdom literature of the Bible. The first of these is called *synonymous parallelism,* and it occurs whenever the psalmist sets forth the same idea twice but in different words. For example:

Lord, *my heart* is *not proud,*
nor are *my eyes haughty* (Ps 131).

My *being proclaims the greatness* of *the Lord* and my *spirit finds joy* in *God* my Savior. (Lk 1:46-47)

The italics bring out the repetition of similar ideas.

A second kind of parallelism works by opposition or contrast, and is called *antithetic parallelism.* Here the second idea contrasts sharply with the first, as in these examples:

He has deposed the mighty from their thrones
    and raised the lowly to high places.
The hungry he has given every good thing,
    while the rich he has sent empty away (Lk 1:52-53).

The method here is to express ideas by contrasting them.

The third type, *synthetic parallelism,* occurs when the second part of the verse combines, expands, develops, or explains the thought of the first part:

When the Lord brought back the captives of Zion,
  we were like men dreaming.

The Lord has done great things for us;
we are glad indeed (Ps 126:1, 3).

Reading carefully, one will note that in almost every psalm there is a blending of parallels, so that it is not uncommon to find all three types—synonymous, antithetic, and synthetic—used in turn. The blending is skillful and enlivens the psalm, avoiding a constant repetition of synonyms or contrast which would soon become monotonous. Here, for example,

(synthetic)   When the Lord brought back the captives of
                   Zion, we were like men dreaming.
(synonymous)   Then was our mouth filled with laughter,
                   and our tongue with exultation.
(antithetic)   Those that sow in tears
                   shall reap rejoicing (Ps 126:1, 2, 6).

It was a great blessing for translators that the scholars discovered the law of parallelism and sorted out the different kinds of parallels. It meant that once the translator had done one line, he generally had a good idea of what he might find in the next line. To show how this works out in practice, look at Psalm 76:2. There the Latin had:

In peace is his tabernacle,
and his abode is Zion.

It is clear that "abode" means "house" or "Temple," "Zion" means "Jerusalem," and "tabernacle" means a "dwelling place" or "tent." But the term ."in peace" is not clear. However, since "abode" and "tabernacle" match, "Zion" and "peace" should match, and indeed, in Hebrew the reading is: *b. shalem sukko.* *Shalem* is the abridged name of *Jerusalem*, called sometimes the "city of peace" (Gn 14:18; Jdt 4:4). Thanks to parallelism, then it is clear that we should translate the verse:

> In Salem is his abode,
> his dwelling is in Zion.

Now try reading the Psalms, or Job, or Proverbs, and the other poetic books, with your mind alert to spot the parallelisms. Today we are fortunate in that the new translations make the task easier, both by the way the poetry is set up, and by a better understanding of the Hebrew language. Many readers of the Bible assemble their own lists of favorite passages.

> Better a dish of herbs when love is there
> than a fatted ox and hatred with it (Prv 15:17).

> Better a dry crust with peace
> than a house full of feasting with strife (17:1).

After you have grown accustomed to parallelism, read some of the wisdom literature for the sheer enjoyment of the parallels. Some are quite striking:

> The race is not won by the swift, nor the battle by the valiant
>   (Qoh 9:11).
> A live dog is better off than a dead lion (v. 4).

> One who pays heed to the wind will not sow,
> and one who watches the clouds will never reap (11:4).

Go to the ant, O sluggard,
study her ways and learn wisdom (Prv 6:6).

What you have not saved in your youth,
how will you acquire in your old age? (Sir 25:3)

A mild answer calms wrath,
but a harsh word stirs up anger (Prv 15:1).

They shall beat their swords into plowshares
and their spears into pruning hooks (Is 2:4).

The Psalms

The book of Psalms (in Hebrew: *tehillim*) is one of the best known and most loved books of the Bible. It is the prayerbook of the Old Testament. The world "psalm" comes from a Greek word meaning "to strike or play on a stringed instrument." Psalms were meant to be sung to music. *Tehillim* means "praises." After almost 3000 years, the psalms are still used by Jew and Christian alike in praise of God.

Those who prefer to be more "modern" find the age of the psalms a liability rather than an asset. But the psalms have survived because they are self-validating, and have a time-resistant quality about them, a kind of universality. They reflect, mirror, express, translate into words all the sentiments of which the human heart is capable; they are sounding boards of the human heart. Moreover, they say what we want to say about or to God, or, perhaps, what we would want to say about him and to him if we had deeper spiritual insight. Being rather unimaginative and uneloquent ourselves, we can make use of these inspired songs to praise God in an excellent way. If we are not sure that the psalms are absolutely the best praise and worship, we can at least be sure that if we pray with the psalms, God will be well-praised, and well-honored. There is reason for the Church's long friendship with the songs of Zion. She appreciates their rightness, and beauty, and makes wise use of them in the divine worship. She is also, incidentally, following the best of examples, for the psalms were used by Jesus himself on the cross (Ps 22:1; 31:5), by Mary in her Magnificat, and by the apostles and martyrs.

The psalms are songs of praise. Praise? Yes, but as John Donne said, here below we are merely tuning our instruments.

The Prophetical Literature

The third type of thought which joins the historical-juridical and wisdom traditions in the Old Testament is that of the prophetical literature. Prophecy is quite extensive, constituting one of the three major divisions of the Bible. The prophetic books come second in the Jewish Bible (Tanak) and third in the Greek Bibles (Takan). Included in it are Lamentations, and, in the Septuagint, the book of Baruch, Jeremiah's secretary.

Prophecy is very ancient, and there have always been men, and some women like Deborah and Huldah, who have claimed to speak in God's name. There were the ecstatics, bands of prophets upon whom the spirit might suddenly descend (for an example, see 1 Sm 10). But there were also the famous prophets by vocation—Isaiah, Jeremiah, and Ezekiel among them. They are among the glories of Israel. The word for "prophet"—navi—means "one who has been called" or "one who proclaims." He is the mouthpiece of God, fearlessly proclaiming the "word of God" or "the oracle of the Lord" in many ways. The Bible records their words expressed in bitter denunciation, in sermon, proverb, psalm, love songs, satire, or lament songs.

The prophet's proclamation of the "word of God" was sometimes dramatic and extraordinary (see Is 20:3; Ez 4; 5; 12:17ff; 21:23; 37:15). The prophets were masters of symbolic action (see Jer 19:1-11). In the extravagances of prophets, some moderns have detected madness; but this is surely an extravagant conclusion. The abnormal behavior was a calculated "madness" quite incidental to a prophetic message which was always rational. The Old Testament prophets were men who had experienced their God, who called men to obedience and love, and urged them to see the world—past, present, or future—through God's eyes. Capable of harshness and threats, the prophets were also the consolers of their people.

The prophetical writings cover a period of roughly 300 years, extending from Amos and Micah (750 B.C.) to Obadiah (ca. 450 B.C.). Much prophetical writing is in prose; where poetry occurs, the rules of parallelism apply. Prophetic language is often vivid, crackling with excitement, and always urgent. Although the prophets were men of their own times, they dealt with timeless issues. They were God's spokesmen, the conscience of Israel, and the spiritual guides of their people. Thus we can read them for spiritual nourishment today.

True prophets courageously reminded kings and peoples of their responsibilities, but there were also false prophets who were ready to say what people and kings wanted to hear. How to discern the true from the false prophet was always a problem. Two tests were applied. First, if a prophecy came true, the speaker was seen to be a true prophet. However, the application of this criterion posed a problem at times, for it sometimes took centuries for a prophecy to be proved true. Fortunately there was another test that could be applied at once, namely, whether a prophecy was consistent with Yahwistic teaching. The reader is invited to turn, in this connection, to Jeremiah 28.

After the Exile, the written word of the Law came to outweigh the spoken word of the prophet. Prophecy fell into disuse, and even into disrepute (see Zec 13:1-6).

THREE

THE CANON: THE QUESTION OF BELONGING

Catholics and Protestants once read different Bibles, that is, Catholic Bibles contained seven Old Testament books which were omitted in Protestant Bibles. Today that situation has changed; Bibles prepared under Catholic and Protestant auspices are now widely read on both sides of the fence, a genuine ecumenical gain. The purpose of this chapter is to explain how it came about that some books were admitted into the Bible while others were excluded.

The question just posed is clearly one of great importance. The issue revolves around the canonicity of the books in our Bible. The close bond that links Bible and Church will quickly become evident; it is impossible properly to understand one without the other. Involved too is the thorny question of authority. Who can speak in this matter? The historians? The scholars? The Church? All three have much to contribute, to be sure, but in the end it is the living Church's authority that will prevail, for the Bible is more than an ancient book which fascinates scholars and antiquarians. It is, the Church alone assures us, God's book.

This chapter is intended to give readers an overview of the way our Bible came to be.*

*The Jerome Biblical Commentary (#67) contains a discussion of the question of the canon along with a generous bibliography. We propose only to sketch out the problem and formulate a workable solution.

"Canon" Defined

The word "canon" comes from a term which originally referred to a reed (1 Kgs 14:15). The reed was a tool for measuring, and the word eventually came to mean a fixed rule or guide, a measure of other things. It also stands for the thing that is measured (see 2 Cor 10:13-15; Gal 6:16). After 341 A. D. Church regulations which spelled out established norms of conduct came to be called *canones* or canons.

The word "canon" has passed freely into English. There are canons of good behavior, of etiquette, of astronomy, literature, a canon of the Mass, the list of saints. And then there are the canons of a cathedral (not to be confused with cannons!).

The biblical canon is a collection of books which the Church has accepted as inspired and normative, containing truths which are conducive to salvation. St. Athanasius (367) was the first to use the word "canon" in reference to the Bible; he noted that the canonical books differed from all non-inspired writings.

All canonical books of the Bible are inspired, but the terms are not interchangeable. Some inspired books may not be included in our canon because they have disappeared. We know that two of Paul's letters (see 1 Cor 5:9; 2 Cor 1:15) have not survived, and there may have been others we know nothing about. The official list of inspired writings refers only to those which have survived. Catholics list forty-six such books and letters in the Old Testament and twenty-seven in the New Testament.

The inclusion of a book in the official canon of the Church affirms only the divine origin of that book, and says nothing at all about the author of the book. It was an ancient literary practice to issue books under pseudonyms. The Psalter "of David" or the Wisdom "of Solomon" illustrate the practice. David did not compose all 150 Psalms, nor did Solomon write everything that was attributed to him. The question of authorship is a historical problem, not a religious one, and has to be decided by historical methods. The books listed in the canon are inspired books; a book not so listed is not recognized as being inspired.

Proto and Deuterocanonical

Sixtus of Siena (1520-1569) coined the term "protocanonical" to refer to books of the Bible about which there had never been question. By way of contrast, those books which the Church had included in the canon after long debate he called "deuterocanonical." The term does not suggest that such books suffer from an inferior sort of inspiration, but simply that controversy attended their acceptance by the Church. At times these were also called "ecclesiastical" books, as they make suitable reading for churchgoers. Today, the protocanonical books are generally called the canonical books.

A simple scheme will help keep the terms clear, while introducing another term of some importance.

Those books which

Catholics call	Protestants call
Canonical .... Canonical
Deuterocanonical .... Apocrypha
Apocryphal .... Pseudepigrapha

The second term above—deuterocanonical or apocrypha—includes those books which are responsible for the differences between the Catholic and Protestant Bibles. The terms refer to seven Old Testament books which are included in Catholic Bibles and excluded from Protestant Bibles. They are: Tobit, Judith, Wisdom, Sirach, Baruch, First and Second Maccabees, and parts of Esther and Daniel. The Apocrypha are not the same as apocryphal works—writings which all Christians exclude from the Bible. The term "Apocrypha" refers to the seven disputed books mentioned above. Catholics call them "deuterocanonical."

The term "apocrypha" comes from St. Jerome, who used it in disparaging reference, for in his view the "deuterocanonical" books were "inter apocrypha" or "among the apocrypha." However, when he learned that the African churches were accepting the deuterocanonical books as canonical, Jerome agreed with the decision, and cited them with the introductory formula "God says in the Scriptures," which he used for quotations from the canonical books.

The difference between Catholic and Protestant treatment of the deuterocanonical works is attributable to the different ways the Jews themselves handled these books. The deuterocanonical books are not found in the Hebrew Bible, developed in Palestine, although they were a part of the Jewish-Greek Bible (the LXX or Septuagint) developed in Alexandria among the diaspora Jews as far back as 150 B.C. Jerome included them in the Latin Vulgate (fourth century A.D.) and they appear in English Catholic Bibles. They were in the original King James Version (1611), but were omitted by the Westminster Confession of 1648 as not divinely inspired and therefore "of no authority in the Church of God, nor to be otherwise approved or made use of than any other human writings." The Thirty-Nine Articles, however, made allowance for their restricted use.

Of late there has been an upsurge of interest in these disputed books, which witness to the intertestamental period. To ignore so sizable a corpus of writings from this otherwise little-known period seems unscholarly, to say the least. When Goodspeed and Smith's *Chicago Bible* was reissued as *The Complete Bible* (1923), it contained these seven books together with 1-2 Esdras and the touching Prayer of Manasseh. Since 1957, editions of the *Revised Standard Version* have assigned the deuterocanonical books to a special section. *The New English Bible* (1970) also makes room for them.

The source of this difference lies in diaspora Judaism. Ancient Palestine, a land about the size of the state of Delaware, was too small to provide a good living for all its people, and many of the Jews went elsewhere seeking greener pastures. Jewish settlers did very well in both Egypt and Rome, and they also found homes in Asia Minor and even India. They were described as people of the *diaspora*, a Greek word meaning "scattered ones." Economic and political factors encouraged them to speak Greek, the regional language. The diaspora Jews were of

course constantly exposed to the considerable pressures of
Greek culture. Children born in the diaspora became less and
less familiar with Hebrew, and it was only a matter of time until
Greek was used in the synagogues.

In spite of the distance that separated them, the Jews of the
diaspora and of the homeland were bound together by many
ties. Geographically, Egypt and Israel were neighbors, and
there was much coming and going between the large cities like
Alexandria and Jerusalem. There is nothing to indicate that the
two communities pursued divergent paths in religion; on the
contrary, their tenacity as regards the traditional belief is well
known. When the diaspora Jews wanted their Scriptures in
Greek, it is not at all improbable that Jerusalem itself provided
translators and translations of the sacred books, and that the
deuterocanonical books were both known and used in that city.
The word "canon" was not used, since the question of "belonging" was not crucial at that time.

Why, then, are there differences between the diaspora Greek
Bible and the Hebrew Bible in Palestine? Part of the answer
lies in the eruption of the ancient tension that smoldered between Jew and Greek, between Jewish ways of thought and
those of Greece. This tension surfaced violently during Maccabean times and undoubtedly carried over into the New Testament polemic between Jews and Christians. Semitic decisions
are often all black or all white, either-or, absolute. If Jewish
Christians justified their novel teachings by appealing to a
Greek Bible, a predictable Jewish reaction might have been the
rejection of everything Greek. This may have led to exclusion of
some books found in the Greek-Jewish Bible.

It is difficult to settle the question of the Old Testament
canon on the basis of Jewish practice because the Jews themselves never resolved the question. There is no record of a decision reached by an authoritative Jewish body closing the Old
Testament canon. Each synagogue was autonomous; there was
no central authority comparable to the Roman Catholic Pope.
The jurisdiction of the Sanhedrin was limited, and it was not

Jewish practice to hold councils. A meeting was held at Jamnia (Jabneh, Jabneel) ca. 100 A.D. to discuss certain books, especially Qoholeth and Song of Solomon, but Jamnia was a school rather than a council, and had no legal authority. It neither produced a list of acceptable books, nor did it exclude any books by name.

Naturally, the Jews made "gatherings" of sacred books. First to be "gathered" was the Law. It was soon written down; a copy of it was placed in the Ark (Dt 17:18; 31:26). The songs of David, of Asaph, and of other singers were also assembled. After the Exile, Nehemiah's library contained both the Law and the Prophets. By the time Sirach came to be written, ca. 180 B.C., it was customary to speak of the Law, the Prophets, and the other books. This development was unplanned, and happened slowly. Discussion about the canon continued among the Jews until the late second and early third centuries A.D. By this time, Christians had taken up the question.

The Christian Old Testament

Some have sought to determine the Old Testament canon by the usage of the New Testament: A book was canonical if the New Testament quoted it. But the New Testament does not quote some of the canonical books—Ruth, Qoholeth, Esther, Ezra, Nehemiah, Obadiah, Nahum, and the Song of Songs. The New Testament quotes from the longer Alexandrian Greek canon no less than 350 times, but not one of these quotations is directly from one of the deuterocanonical books. The New Testament only alludes to the deuterocanonical books. But the argument from silence is usually a weak argument, and the silence of the New Testament about the deuterocanonical books is explicable for other reasons. We cannot use the New Testament to determine the canonicity—the inspired quality—of the deuterocanonical books.

With the exception of Melito of Sardis (171 A. D.), writers of the first three centuries treated deuterocanonical books as they did the canonical ones. The Greek Bible was received and used by the Church. In the fourth century a few of the Fathers began to have reservations concerning the "extra" books. Their view is difficult to explain. Perhaps the growing hostility between Christians and Jews had something to do with their attitude.

Some are shocked to learn that the matter of the biblical canon was not resolved until 1546 A.D.—at the Council of Trent. However, Trent was the last of many words on the subject. The North African Councils of Hippo (393) and Carthage (397), as well as Innocent I (405) and the Gelasian Decree (496) had listed the books long before Trent. The popular "back to the Bible" movement of the Reformation prompted the decisive action taken at Trent. The question was settled, incidentally, not so much on historical as on theological grounds: the test of the canon was the Church's own use of the Bible.

The Christian New Testament

At the time of Jesus' death, no such thing as the New Testament existed. He had himself written nothing (except Jn 8:6-8). After the first Easter morning, Jesus' followers began to proclaim his resurrection and to instruct people in his teachings. Letters were written, first by Paul, then by others, to explain the faith and to instruct in right behavior. Accounts of Jesus' words and deeds were written—chance writings, they could be called, for no one thought of writing books about him that would be collected into something called the New Testament. These writings began to coalesce before the end of the first century, molded, colored, and corrected by an oral tradition which insured accuracy. As the apostles and the first generation of Christians began to die, younger believers began to take steps to assemble some more or less permanent record of Jesus and his doctrine. A "corpus" was then in formation.

All this took place sporadically, without much planning or urgency, until the appearance of the heresy of Marcion. On becoming a Christian Marcion also became a fanatic. He argued that since the Old Testament had been fulfilled in Jesus, the New Testament should be divested of anything that smacked of the Old Testament. For his aggressiveness, Marcion achieved the dubious distinction of being the first man ever to be excommunicated by the Church. He also precipitated the formation of the New Testament canon, or official listing of New Testament writings. To combat his heresy, the Church began to ask which of the "sacred" writings were really inspired.

By the end of the second century A.D. (Marcion died ca. 160), the gospels were already in a class by themselves, enjoying a special authority. They were being read in religious assemblies by the middle of the second century, something we have been doing ever since. Paul's writings were soon looked upon as "Scripture" (2 Pt 3:15f); by 100, thirteen of his works were mentioned by name and used in liturgical gatherings (see 1 Thes 5:27; Col 4:16; 2 Cor 2:3ff). Other ancient writings highly esteemed by the early Christians were the Didache, the Shepherd of Hermas, and the letters of Clement, Ignatius, and Barnabas, but none of these were ever considered to be on the same level as the canonical New Testament books.

What we have in the New Testament today has been there since ca. 200 A.D., and was in existence much earlier. By 217 the Egyptian Church acknowledged twenty-seven New Testament books; the Latin and Eastern Churches did the same by the late fourth century. Forming the New Testament was a slow process and, in the end, the canon which took shape was the creation of the Church. Without the Church there would never have been a canon; it was the Church's interest to select from many writings those which reflected and best expressed her faith. However, the Jesus of the New Testament is not a pre-Christian Jesus; he is, rather, the Jesus to whom the Christian Church was the response.

Important as the question of the canon may be, it is pretty much a settled one. What is not clear is the precise reason why certain books were accepted and others rejected. Jesus and the apostles used and approved the Old Testament; Paul's letters were put on a par with the Old Testament by 2 Peter, and it was the Church alone that approved the gospels and other writings.

Her decision was at least in part linked with the matter of apostolicity—all the New Testament writings in one way or another have an apostolic origin. The Church's choice was also governed by conformity to the community's rule of faith.

In conclusion, the question of the canon of the Bible is more than a historical matter. For some, the Bible needs no justification; it stands by itself. For Roman Catholics, the Church's voice is the deciding factor. This statement is not meant to minimize the importance or validity of historical and scholarly criticism, but is simply an affirmation that the question is at bottom a religious one.

The Apocryphal Writings

For all its excellence, the Bible can be an exasperating book that often leaves its readers wondering what happened next. For example, Adam and Eve were driven from Paradise by an angel with a fiery sword, but then ... ? Aside from a few genealogies, the early story of man ends there. Again, Enoch, who walked with God, vanished because God took him. Yes, yes, the reader says to himself breathlessly, what happened, and how? No answer is forthcoming. The Old Testament is filled with loose ends.

To tie up these loose ends, a vast literature came into being during the troubled period from 200 B.C. to 100 A.D. We might call this a "people's literature." Its aims were to fill in the chinks in the Bible story, and also to make life endurable under trying circumstances. Life was hard in those days, especially for a proud people chafing under a foreign domination. The Chosen People knew what forced labor, heavy taxes, humiliation, and derision meant, and it was rendered the more bitter because they could remember when David and Solomon ruled in splendor and worshiped God in his holy Temple in Jerusalem. They longed for the return of those days, or rather, for the coming of the great day when a promised liberator would lead them to victory over all their foes. On that glorious day the world would see vindication, justice, revenge, and the humiliation of the oppressor.

The apocryphal literature arose in this atmosphere. It was a crisis literature and, at the same time, a kind of safety-valve, a source of hope. It was a kind of religious writing in which the value of prayer, the beauty of temperance and chastity and other virtues were emphasized, and the dangers of certain types of sin recognized.

I once ran across a newspaper item explaining that the apocryphal writings were those which for centuries had been gathered up and locked away in the Vatican Library because, if allowed to circulate, they would expose the intrinsic wickedness and corruption of the Church. The writer had obviously never read either the apocrypha or any of the many books which discuss them. He would soon have learned that these writings are as a rule wearisome and tedious, and that the ancient decision to exclude them from the canon was a wise one. The great biblical scholar, St. Jerome, took a dim view of the apocrypha and of the people who preferred to drink from muddy waters, rather than from the pure waters of the spring (i.e., the gospels).

We spend some time discussing the apocrypha because knowledge of this material helps a reader better understand and appreciate the Bible itself. The apocrypha shed an indirect light on the Bible. Indirectly they tell us that the Bible is *not* an answer book, that we do not know everything, that the Bible is a special kind of history which deals soberly with the great basic ideas: God, man, sin, and God's saving activity. More specifically the apocrypha record the imaginings, hopes, and fears of the men who wrote and read them. Through them we learn what interested them, the ideals they cherished and admired.

The Church has now and then borrowed a phrase or sentence from the apocrypha. The entrance antiphon *(Requiem aeternam . . .)* of a Requiem Mass, for example, is from 4 Esdras. But such usage is the exception. No article of belief has originated in the apocrypha. Periodically, movements are launched to purge the liturgy of apocryphal borrowings—efforts which meet with only partial success. Man's longing for the tangible and concrete, for answers to his questions, runs deep and cannot easily be denied.

Indeed, the apocrypha have exercised so great an influence throughout the ages that no one who is interested in the history of Christian thought and art can afford to neglect them. Great artists went to them for inspiration. Michelangelo adorned the ceiling of the Sistine Chapel with Sibyls. Dante modeled his famous journey through hell, purgatory, and heaven on the *Book of Enoch*. Song writers have rhapsodized about the Seventh Heaven, and movie makers have successfully dramatized apocryphal stories like *Quo Vadis* and *The Robe*. Milton too borrowed a theme from *Enoch* and *Jubilees*, both of which elaborated the curious text of Genesis 6:1-4. In our own times, modern witches and wizards are wont to invoke the names of the fallen angels, which are only recorded in *Enoch*, an apocryphal work.

It thus behooves the educated Bible reader to know something about the apocrypha. This knowledge will enable us to recognize the source of some themes of our culture. By considering the apocrypha, we will also better appreciate the impressive restraint and sobriety of the canonical writings.

The later Jewish rabbis called the apocrypha "the outside books," but in some circles they were the "inside books," that is, to the Gnostics and others who boasted of esoteric and secret writings (see Dn 12:9-10). The very word *apocrypha* means "secret" or "hidden"; our words "crypt" and "cryptic" retain this meaning. In days of old, as in many lands today, swift and savage official reprisals forced people to speak and write about those in authority with care, in veiled language. The apocrypha did just that. (So does the New Testament. See 1 Pt 5:13 where St. Peter refers to Rome as Babylon.)

And now for a look at some of these interesting writings.

Old Testament Apocrypha

The Book of Enoch. This work, one of the most popular and by far the most important of all apocryphal books, sheds much light on Jewish theology in the second century B.C. It includes a description of Enoch's translation by God to heaven (Gn 5:24; Sir 44:16), and of his journeys through earth and Sheol (1:17-36). It provides the names of twenty of the two hundred fallen angels, and describes their fall (see Gn 6). Enoch discusses astronomical and calendrical matters, the Flood, and presents visions of men in animal form. It sees the world, now in its seventh week, as having three weeks to go until the end and the final victory of the just. *Enoch* was much esteemed in Christian circles because of its messianic and eschatological tone (v. 14 of the letter of Jude refers to it), and in it for the first time are references to the Son of Man, to the Messiah, the Chosen One who is also the Righteous One.

Jubilees or *Little Genesis.* This work, written about 100 B.C., presents an alternate view of man's origins and destiny. It contains such Pharisaic ideas as human liberty, free will, and moral accountability for one's actions. Adam's fall is said to have affected only himself and the animals, and was paid for by the Deluge. The subsequent wickedness of the human race is attributed to the seduction of the daughters of men by the sons of God (i.e., angels) and demonic spirits. (A recent use of this idea is the film *Rosemary's Baby.*) The Law is considered to be of eternal validity; but, prophetism has ceased forever. The Messiah to come will be from Judah and of the Maccabean line. All hope of a resurrection of the body is abandoned; the blessed will be immortal souls only. After lasting 1000 years, the messianic kingdom will come to an end with the final judgment.

4 Esdras (= 2 Esdras). This work was widely read in the early Church. It is an ascetic work (ca. 70-100 A.D.) in which certain agonizing problems are taken up: why Israel must suffer so much, why so few are saved, what the coming world will be like, and details about the Messiah. There one encounters references to the Son of Man, and beautiful passages on the love of God and the Law. In the *New English Bible,* 1-2 Esdras (also numbered 3-4 Esdras) are included, as is the *Prayer of Manasseh,* a short (15 vv.) penitential psalm telling of the infinite compassion of God and of the effectiveness of true repentance and prayer. It is probably one of the best pieces in the apocrypha.

Other Old Testament Apocrypha. The Sibyl (a pre-Homeric fiction) appears in the *Sibylline Oracles* (second century B.C.) as Noah's daughter-in-law. The Oracles might otherwise be forgotten were it not for Michelangelo, and for the Sequence in the Mass of the Dead, the *Dies irae ... teste David cum Sibylla.*

The *Testament of the Twelve Patriarchs* is a takeoff on Genesis 49 and once enjoyed a great vogue in the Church, being the most ethical of all the Old Testament apocrypha. Pius XI's famous remark, "spiritually we are all Semites" echoed the sentiment expressed in the *Testament* that the Gentiles will be saved through Israel. *4 Maccabees* (ca. 70 A.D.) develops an important theme—the value of vicarious sufferings. It also presents belief in immortality. Satan's contending with Michael for the body of Moses appears in the *Assumption of Moses* (see Jude 9).

New Testament Apocrypha

There is a vast New Testament apocryphal literature, prompted by the brevity of the New Testament writings. Characteristic of such writings is their abundance of detail, especially in the matter of names. Given the treasure that we have in the authentic writings, there is perhaps less reason for tarrying over the New Testament apocrypha than there was for the Old Testament apocrypha.

However, there is one very good reason for taking a brief look at some of the New Testament apocrypha: to a greater extent than is proper, much popular devotion has roots in these apocryphal writings. Things that "everybody knows for a fact" have no other historical basis than some apocryphal writing. These "facts" include: the names of Mary's parents, Joachim and Anna; the idea that Mary was sixteen years old when she became Joseph's wife; the idea that Joseph was an older man, father of sons, and a widower; and the story that he was chosen to be Mary's spouse because his staff burst into bloom (an image reproduced in countless statues of St. Joseph). Generations of Christians were taught that the names of the two thieves on the cross were Dismas and Gestas (or Titus and Dumachus), and that as an infant Dismas had been restored to health by being bathed in water that had washed the child Jesus. The apocrypha supply details of Jesus' childhood in abundance. What he looked like as a grown man is found in a *Letter of Lentulus*, a work which contains the unlikely statement that Jesus had "often been seen to weep, but no man ever saw him laugh."

In the apocryphal *Acts* one can also find things "everybody knows." The *Acts of Peter* tells the *Quo Vadis* story, and contains the information that Peter was at his own request crucified upside down. Before that, there is the diverting but more than slightly ridiculous story of how Peter made a camel go back and forth through the eye of a (very small) needle. The *Acts of Paul* contains, along with many other things, the story of Paul and Thecla, long a European favorite. As for Veronica, who wiped the face of Jesus with a towel and found it imprinted with Jesus' portrait, she and the towel are found only in the apocryphal *Acts of Pilate*. One is not surprised to learn from this source that Veronica was the woman who had been cured of a flow of blood by touching the hem of Jesus' garment.

From what has been sampled here, we can see that St. Jerome was right. We have no need to drink the muddied waters, when the pure clean spring is available.

FOUR

INSPIRATION

Sooner or later, Bible readers find themselves asking questions about the Bible. What makes this book so special? Why is it in a class by itself? Is it the contents, or the claims of its authors? Is it to be accepted on its own merits? Does the Church have anything to say in the matter? Intriguing questions, all of them heavy with historical and theological overtones, and all rewarding.

Contents

Everyone who has read the Bible notes something special about it. The scholar, J. B. Phillips, sensing the vitality and power of the Bible, put it well when he said, "The Bible is in quite a special sense, inspired. It is not magical nor is it faultless; human beings wrote it. But by something which I would not hesitate to describe as a miracle, there is a concentration upon that area of inner truth which is fundamental and ageless. That, I believe, is the reason why millions of people have heard the voice of God speaking to them through these seemingly artless pages."

The Bible emanates light and warmth, true enough. It sketches out God's loving care for his children. Who has not thrilled to the words of Psalm 23, "The Lord is my shepherd?" Or been touched by Ruth's plea to Naomi, one of the most beautiful passages in all Scripture: "Do not ask me to abandon or forsake you, for wherever you go I will go, wherever you lodge I will lodge. Your people shall be my people, and your God, my God" (Ru 1:16). David's lament over the deaths of Jonathan and Saul evoke a familiar sadness (2 Sm 1:19-27), and Solomon's humble prayer for wisdom still arouses feelings of nobility and reverence (1 Kgs 3:3-9). The New Testament also contains many lovely passages which corroborate the view that the Bible is an inspiring book.

While acknowledging the beauty and power of many a page in the Bible, one must not close one's eyes to other facts. There are many places in the Bible which are no more inspiring than a phonebook. The Bible has its own Gobi deserts (see Jos 15-21) and dark valleys (passages where its heroes display disappointingly human weaknesses, as in the story of David and Bathsheba in 2 Sm 11-12). Many a reader has gone to the Bible in search of instruction, comfort, and guidance, and been shocked instead at what he found. For example, Jephthah, one of the judges, offers up his own daughter as a human sacrifice (Jgs 11). Or consider Lamech's murderous policy to destroy anyone, man or boy, who crossed him. The law of retaliation (the *lex talionis*) demands "an eye for an eye, a tooth for a tooth" (Ex 21:23-25), and the holy war (or *herem*) aimed at the total extermination of the enemy (Nm 31; Jos 11:20; 1 Sm 15:1-3). Elisha's reaction when taunted by some "teen-agers" surpasses understanding (2 Kgs 2:23f), and it is likewise distressing to find the prayerbook of the Old Testament, the book of Psalms, ringing with pleas for vengeance, or shouts of satisfaction at the downfall of one's enemies (see Ps 109:6-19; 137:9). Can these pages have a place in the Bible? They can, and do.

The above examples are all from the Old Testament, but the gospels provide many surprises too. Jesus directs angry words at the religious leaders of his people, and he curses a fig tree for not bearing fruit when it was not the season for fruit (see Mt 23; 21:18f). James and John suggested to the Lord that the Samaritans be punished by a rain of fire (Lk 9:54), and Paul "bragged" about his accomplishments (2 Cor 11). None of this fits readily into a category of "pious reading." The inspired book is not always inspirational.

How do we know that the Bible is inspired? *Not* by its contents. Well, then, what if the authors of the various books said they were inspired by God?

Authors' Claims

Throughout the Old Testament, the "spirit of the Lord" *(ruah Yahweh)* came upon men, giving them unusual powers such as skills (Ex 31:2ff) or prophecy (1 Sm 19:20). But the biblical authors seem for the most part to have been unaware that they were being guided by God in their writing (see 2 Mc 2:26ff). They were hard-working men whose message was not precoded for them. Philo's poetic description of the sacred writers as "lyres struck by the unseen hand of God" would have sounded as strange to them as it does to us.

A question often hotly debated is how God can move a man to do what God wants without trespassing upon or destroying the man's liberty. There is a very interesting philosophical and theological point here. God is all-powerful and all-wise, but man is also free. Can the two truths be reconciled? Yes, at least up to a point. After much theological thought on the matter, it has been perceived and stated, with exquisite precision, that God moves free beings—men and angels—freely, that is, according to their natures. This he does by a movement that is at once intrinsically declinable, and yet infallibly efficacious. A marvellous statement, respectful of both the mystery and the facts as we know them.

Internal and Comparative Evidence

We come somewhat closer to a definition of inspiration by looking at the Scriptures themselves. How do they compare to other holy works? What does Scripture itself say about inspiration?

Thanks to archaeology, long-lost libraries now provide us with a vast religious literature whose very existence was hitherto unknown. Today we have a considerable corpus of religious writings from ancient times, and we are no longer surprised to learn that similarities exist between other religious epics and those in the Bible. After all, the Bible grew from within polytheism, amid conflicting views about God and the universe and man. However, it can be said with confidence that the Bible stands alone in its lofty view of God. Only in Israel was there one God; he alone was without a consort; only he was loving and personal and had made a covenant with a chosen people. The Old Testament concept of a servant of the Lord who would suffer for the sins of others is unique in ancient literature. And only in the Bible is the problem of good and evil given a half-way decent explanation.

The Bible is similarly distinctive when compared with other holy works. Mohammed (571-632), the founder of Islam or the Moslem religion, wrote (i.e., dictated) the Koran, the holy book of the Arab world. In its 114 *surahs*, there is outlined a definite way of life—prayer, alms, fasting, pilgrimage to Mecca, and the profession of the faith—that leads infallibly to eternal bliss. This way of life still influences millions of people. The Moslems believe that the Koran is holy, but others view skeptically a writing which resulted from Mohammed's repeated ecstasies or trances, and which contains an odd mixture of the Old Testament, the New Testament, and folklore.

The best-known American holy book is *The Book of Mormon*, the scripture of the Mormon religion. Joseph Smith (d. 1841), founder of the Church of Jesus Christ of Latter Day Saints, claimed he had discovered some golden tablets upon which there was a writing he alone could read, thanks to the magic spectacles named Urim and Thummim (see Ex 28:30) given him by the angel Moroni. Written in "Reformed Egyptian" these tablets spoke of the pre-Columbian Indians of North and South America; according to Smith, these Indians were actually the descendants of the ancient lost tribes of Israel.

Smith's followers eventually expressed a desire to see the tablets which contained such wonderful things. At first, Smith was unwilling to permit this, but in the end a select few were allowed to gaze from the doorway at a table upon which the tablets, covered by a cloth, were resting. The next day Smith informed his followers that the tablets had been taken back to heaven; the angel had been displeased at their lack of faith.

Are Smith's writings "holy" writings? The Book of Mormon is a hodgepodge of the New Testament (the text used is that of the King James Version), and contains many anachronisms, contradictions, a bit of Shakespeare, and standard Campbellite answers to theological problems current in the early nineteenth century. It can hardly be equated with the Bible.

Finally, what does the Bible itself say about its own inspiration? For Jesus and his disciples, the sacred writings were what we call the Old Testament. They referred to these scriptures as "God's word" (see Mt 22:31; Acts 1:16; 4:25; Rom 3:2; 1 Cor 14:31; Heb 33:7). One could hardly hope for a stronger recommendation. The problem is that we know these writings did not suddenly appear, but rather, were laboriously produced by human hands and minds. Two passages in the New Testament touch upon this:

All Scripture is inspired of God and is useful for teaching, for reproof, correction, and training in holiness, so that the man of God may be fully competent and equipped for every good work" (2 Tm 3:16). [The Greek word for "inspired" used here is *theopneustos,* meaning "God-breathed" or inspired.]

There is no prophecy contained in Scripture which is a personal interpretation. No prophecy has ever been put forward by man's willing it. It is rather that men, impelled by the holy Spirit [*theopheromenoi:* "God-borne"], have spoken under God's influence" (2 Pt 1:21).

However, these passages refer clearly only to the Old Testament and to those parts of the New Testament which had by then been written. Thus a problem remains, for one cannot prove the Scriptures by quoting the Scriptures. They are not self-validating. Some assurance must come to us from another outside source. The Church is such a source.

The Church and the Bible

Christians too are a People of the Book. The Bible is more at home in the Church than in a scholar's study. One can imagine such a study without the Bible, but one cannot picture the Bible, especially the New Testament, without the Church. The Bible and the Church go together. Both are objects of faith, not of mathematical or historical or linguistic proof. Faith is not the result, nor the function, of any of these sciences; it is both a gift and a duty.

The Church is resolutely biblical. Presiding at the birth of the New Testament, and accepting it along with the Old Testament, the Church is responsible for the formation of the canon. She has always venerated the divine Scriptures, just as she has venerated the body of the Lord, unceasingly receiving and offering to the faithful the bread of life. For her, the Bible is *the word of God* and it receives special attention and courtesy. At liturgical gatherings the Bible is enthroned upon altars, is reverently kissed, and enveloped by clouds of incense.

The Bible is proclaimed in the Church, and by the Church. So intimate is the union between the Church and the Scriptures that no true opposition between the two is possible. It accepts the Bible as the word of God not because of its contents, nor because of claims made by its writers, nor because it is inspiring, but simply and solely because of the Church's assurance that the Scriptures are in fact God's word. There is no other alternative. The Church proclaims the Bible to the world as a sacred writing that contains everything God wanted written down, especially that truth which God wanted put into writing for the sake of our salvation. We accept this assurance gratefully, with full awareness that what we are doing is an act of faith.

Church Statements on Inspiration

The immense value of Church guidance in matters biblical will become clearer from the following review of official statements issued by the Church as she both lives out the Bible in her daily life, and reacts to the pressures and needs of an ever-changing world. Obviously, guidance is necessary; no less a genius than St. Augustine declared that he "would not even accept the gospels, were it not for the authority of the Church." He was right in this, as we shall see.

The word "inspire" appears for the first time in an ecclesiastical document in 1441 when the Council of Florence declared its conviction that one and the same God was author of both the Old and the New Testaments. The Council said that all the books, which it listed one by one, were composed by men (*sancti*) of both Testaments who spoke under the inspiration of the Holy Spirit *(Spiritu Sancto inspirante)*.

In the wake of the Reformation, as we have seen (Chapter Three) the Council of Trent faced the problem of the canon and in 1546 decisively settled that question. Trent listed all the books of both the Old and the New Testaments—the deuterocanonical books included—which were authored by God. Trent's position was reaffirmed by the First Vatican Council (1870). Vatican I also clarified the notion of canonicity: this is the Church's acknowledgement of books which were written under the inspiration of the Holy Spirit.

An encyclical issued by Pope Leo XIII in 1893 inaugurated a new era in Catholic biblical studies. The *Providentissimus Deus* contained a clear description of biblical inspiration:

God by supernatural power so moved and impelled the human authors to write, and so assisted them when writing, that the things he ordered and those only they first rightly understood, then willed faithfully to write down, and finally expressed in apt words and with infallible truth.

The *Spiritus Paraclitus* (1920) was issued on the 1500th an-niversary of the death of St. Jerome, the patron of biblical studies. In it, Benedict XV remarked that Leo's words about in-spiration were traditional. Long ago Jerome had taught that God was the author of the Scriptures, that he moved and prodded the will of the sacred author and remained with him until he finished the task. Benedict also insisted that in the Bible there was true history, not just hearsay or make-believe.

Rome loves anniversaries. In 1943, on the fiftieth anniversary of Leo's great biblical encyclical, Pius XII released his *Divino Afflante Spiritu*. It ratified much of what Leo said, but showed an awareness of what had happened in the half-century since his time. The men who wrote the Bible were true authors, liv-ing instruments of the Holy Spirit. The Pope urged biblical scholars to study the original texts—the Hebrew and Greek, and not just the Latin Vulgate, which Trent had so warmly recom-mended. In a bold step forward, *Divino Afflante* endorsed the study of literary forms, and urged scholars to venture forth into the difficult areas of biblical research. A bold step indeed; a door opening outward to the future. The dynamic Church wants no "Exegetes who major issues shun/ And hold their farthing candles to the sun" (Alexander Pope).

The statement that "all things are the sum of their past" applies in a special way to that venerable institution, the Church. The nineteenth century saw rationalism, liberalism, and anti-clericalism flourish as never before. Religion and its sacred writings became targets of attack. Archaeology had sparked a furious activity in historical and linguistic circles which climaxed in the successful decipherment of hieroglyphic and cuneiform writings. Anthropology (Darwin), psychology (Freud), and geology contributed to the general intellectual ferment sparked by these ancient writings. As civilizations and literatures older than or contemporary with Israel emerged from the dust, numerous parallels between its laws and customs and those of other peoples appeared, and it became evident that the Bible was not as original a book as many had believed. Questions followed. Did Adam and Eve (one pair, or many?) ever exist? How old is man and his world? What is man's relation to the apes? The early chapters of Genesis became, in a relatively short time, a source of embarrassment for many; and of fear also, for if errors could be detected in these chapters, how long would it be before they would be found elsewhere, even in the gospels?

In such controversies, the Church's position has generally been one of caution. Caution is not popular in excited times, but it is sound policy. Chesterton once described an impetuous man who leaped upon his horse and galloped furiously off in all directions. Not the Church. At Vatican II, three urgent problems were given a prolonged scrutiny: (1) The relationship between Scripture and Tradition; (2) the impact of modern critical historical methods upon the Bible; and (3) the modern biblical movement. The results appear in the Council document *Dei Verbum,* the *Constitution on Divine Revelation.*

The *Dei Verbum*

The *Constitution on Divine Revelation,* one of the great documents to emerge from Vatican II, was approved by a vote of 2,344 to 6 on November 11, 1965. Its gradual evolution is a matter of public record, thanks to the coverage given to the Council and its proceedings by the news media. Two Popes intervened in the discussion of this document in a significant way. On November 21, 1962, Pope John XXIII turned the first draft of the document on revelation over to a new committee, although according to the rules of procedure he need not have done so. This prompted a Protestant observer at the Council to declare that "for the first time in my life, I see the value of a pope!" The second intervention came on December 4, 1963, when Paul VI ordered the controversial draft on revelation to be put on the agenda for the third (1964) session of the Council. Two years later, the *Dei Verbum* appeared. Thus it was in the making throughout the entire "life" of the Council. From that one fact one can begin to see how important a document it is.

The *Dei Verbum* derives its name from the opening words, which come from Isaiah 40:8: "The word of our God abides forever." The phrase recurs in Chapter three and again in the last paragraph of Chapter six. After a short preface, there follow six chapters. Thus:

Preface (1)
1 Revelation Itself (2-6)
2 The Transmission of Divine Revelation (7-10)
3 Divine Inspiration and the Interpretation of Sacred Scripture (11-13)
4 The Old Testament (14-16)
5 The New Testament (17-20)
6 Sacred Scripture in the Life of the Church (21-26)

The numbers in parentheses indicate sections within the chapters and are referred to as "articles." There is one chapter on Revelation, one on Tradition, and four on Scripture.

The *Dei Verbum* bears some marks of the tensions and clashes amid which it was forged, but on the whole it is a synthesis of great value. Far from being a mere rehash of things said before, it is a remarkable example of how loyalty to Tradition can be fruitfully combined with openness to critical scholarship. It is a pastoral document, motivated by a positive care for the modern believer. The term "pastoral" has nothing to do with forests and glens and nymphs (as in literature), but refers to the care a shepherd (*pastor,* in Latin) has for his flock. It suggests an openness to discussion, and the use both of scriptural language and modern, contemporary modes of expression. The *Dei Verbum* is a rich lode that will be mined for years to come as successive generations endeavor to penetrate more deeply into the meaning of revelation, Tradition, the Bible, and the Church.

Let us examine in summary form some of the most important ideas in *Dei Verbum*.

Revelation

Revelation is an "unveiling of God." This is something only God can do, but he has done it so that man would realize that he had a plan for the salvation of man. Revelation is a divine-human dialogue with its roots in history. In the Hebrew language, "word" and "thing" (or "event") are interchangeable terms. The Christmas shepherds resolved to go to Bethlehem "to see this *word* that has come to pass." God's disclosure of himself was effected in and through historical events. Israel understood, from the fact that God punished man for his sins, that he was a moral God. By the Exodus and desert experience, Israel saw that he was a provident God. By being saved from mighty foes, Israel came to understand that he was a saving God. The climax of revelation was Jesus himself, the very Word of God, the one in whom God has now said everything that is to be said about himself. So magnificent a revelation cannot and will not be added to until the moment when the Lord Jesus shall return in glory.

The initiative for all divine disclosure rests with God. Man's acceptance of it, his "Yes" to God, is not, however, a purely static reception of revelation. He receives it in a human way— that is, God's gift *(donum)* calls for a corresponding act of belief *(opus)*. There is something for man to do, and he must maintain an openness to God however he may be encountered, whether in the future, in history, or in the preaching of the Church.

Revelation is said to have ceased with the death of the last apostle, but this must be understood: with the help of the Holy Spirit, the believer penetrates ever more deeply into the revelation which has been made. Individual experiences of God (i.e., private revelations such as Lourdes or Fatima or Guadalupe) have always to be measured by what God has already said. "Philip, he who sees me, has seen the Father" (Jn 14:9).

Tradition

How can one learn about God's revelation, and what it is that God has revealed? First of all, through Jesus himself, and then by the apostles who preached what they had learned from Jesus and from living with him. God revealed something far transcending mere explicit statements in words. The Holy Spirit saw to it that the commission to preach was fulfilled as well by those apostles and apostolic men (Mark and Luke, for example, were not themselves apostles) who committed the message of salvation to writing. The apostles left behind them successors or bishops—men with authority to teach. So closely, then, do Tradition, Scripture, and the Church go together that one cannot stand without the others.

Not all agree with this statement, and *sola scriptura* (Scripture *alone*) became a Reformer battle cry. But the deep issues at stake cannot be resolved by making the Bible a "paper pope." Tradition and Scripture are like a mirror in which the pilgrim Church on earth looks at God; both of these, flowing from the same wellspring, in a certain way merge into a unity and tend to the same end.

Tradition is not necessarily static, and, with the help of the Holy Spirit, apostolic tradition develops in the Church. Being herself measured by revelation, the Church cannot add to it. Growth in Tradition means, therefore, an increasing understanding of something real which has been given from the start. Tradition is not only a memory of the past but something better—a deeper understanding of the past. The living teaching office of the Church (the Magisterium) is charged with the task of interpreting God's word, but the Church is not above that word; she is not the custodian, but the servant of God's word, to which she must always listen and obey.

Nevertheless, it is not from Scripture alone that the Church draws her certainty about what has been revealed. Such certitude comes from the inner testimony of the Spirit. Nor is that task one proper to the hierarchy alone, for the work of preserving and realizing the word of God concerns the whole people of God.

One of Tradition's major achievements was the settling of the canon. Through these writings, progressively understood and lived, God continually converses with the Bride of Christ.

Thus neither Tradition nor revelation are a "set of propositions" to be believed in and acted upon. Tradition is a dynamic realization of faith, faith-in-action, the process whereby the sacred writings become a real conversation between God and man.

Inspiration

The *Dei Verbum* endorsed the traditional view of inspiration by saying that "the divinely revealed realities which are contained and presented in Sacred Scripture have been committed to writing under the inspiration of the Holy Spirit." But Vatican II went far beyond anything previously stated when it viewed the Bible as, in a special way, "the vessel of the divine revelation of salvation," as the extraordinary writing that preserves revelation, and makes it available for men to assimilate.

Vatican II marked a progress beyond the *Divino Afflante*. That encyclical called the human authors "living instruments." *Dei Verbum*, by contrast, called the sacred writers "true authors." The personal emphasis is important. God is no longer described as the principal author of the Bible, but is recognized as having exercised a true influence on the sacred writers. These men, using their various talents in their own highly personal ways, in the end produced the very book God wanted produced.

Augustine once observed that God wanted to make men Christians, not mathematicians, and that the Holy Spirit had no intention of teaching men things that were not helpful for salvation. Vatican II quotes Aquinas writing in the same vein: "Things which cannot affect our salvation do not belong to inspiration." These momentous words contained a long-sought-for way out of an impasse concerning the Bible and truth.

On October 2, 1964, Cardinal König raised the issue of the Bible and factual accuracy on the floor of the Council. He said that in the Bible, historical and scientific items were sometimes wrong. He brought up factual errors: Mk 2:26 says David ate the holy bread when Abiathar was highpriest (the correct name is

Abimelech); Mt 27:9 ascribes a prophecy to Jeremiah (it should be Zechariah); Dn 1:1 gives a wrong date. There are other examples known to scholars. The geography and chronology in Daniel, Tobit, Judith, and Esther can often be questioned, and the theology of Job 14:14-22 clearly contradicts New Testament revelation. However, *Dei Verbum* points out that none of these deficiencies are connected with the message itself.

> Since everything asserted by the inspired authors or sacred writers must be held to be asserted by the Holy Spirit, it follows that the books of Scripture must be acknowledged as teaching firmly, faithfully, and without error, that truth which God wanted put into the sacred writings for the sake of our salvation.

Note that the text speaks of *truth* but not of *truths*. It refers to the truth which God *wanted* put into writing, but not that *he put* it in writing. The human author is not shunted into the background. Thus the profound nature of Scripture appears: it is the product of God and of man, a joint activity wherein each maintains his own autonomy. This means that the message of salvation is embedded in history, and that the message may arrive accompanied by something less than perfection. However, God sees to it that the truth of salvation is surely and faithfully taught without error (see 2 Tm 3:16f).

Interpretation

The perfect guide to the understanding of the Bible is the Holy Spirit, under whose guidance the reader should address himself not just to the isolated and obscure passages, but to the Scriptures as a whole. In the last analysis, however, it is the Church's voice that will count. It is reassuring to see the Church making the Bible easily available to all, while affirming the value of Tradition and warmly recommending the ancient versions of both the East and the West.

The work of interpretation falls necessarily to exegetes. They are ministers of the word and servants of the Church. Vatican II gently reminded them that they are not the only ones seeking to understand the Scriptures; the Church also seeks that knowledge. The Church is eager to assimilate scientific knowledge and to organize it through that intimate "knowing" of God which is called theology. Biblical scholars are encouraged to pursue their work in collaboration with theologians, using all fitting means to provide nourishment for the people of God under the Church's watchful care. (There is an interesting choice of words here in the *Dei Verbum: care* translates *vigilantia*, a word chosen in preference to *direction*, or *sub ductu*. Once again, that respect for scholarship by the Magisterium, or teaching office of the Church.)

A true scholar will not waste time breaking down open doors, but prefers to tackle difficult and more rewarding subjects, even though that course of action will not infrequently land him in trouble. Critical historical work in Bible areas always generates tensions between various levels in the believing community, but that is something that has to be accepted and lived with as one of the hazards of progress (see Chapter Ten).

Let us now look at what these scholars have learned about the history of the Bible. We will pay special attention to the story of how the Bible has been translated into other languages, including English.

FIVE

THE BIBLE
THROUGH THE AGES

The various books of the Bible were composed in different languages—Hebrew, Aramaic, and Greek. The originals, all now lost, are called "autographs." The translations of them are called "versions." It is time now to look back across history to see how the word of God found expression in the tongues of men. In the course of these pages we shall make the acquaintance of many remarkable men and their work. They are voices of a noble tradition which is ours, and we should appreciate what they have done in the service of the Lord.

The Greek Versions

The Septuagint, or LXX

The *Letter of Aristeas* is a well-known forgery, but it speaks of the origin of the Septuagint and, while beguiling us with blarney, bears witness to an important fact. This briefly is the story. The Egyptian ruler Ptolemy Philadelphus (285-246 B.C.), at the urging of his Athenian librarian Demetrius, experienced a royal desire to fill out his magnificent library at Alexandria (it once boasted 600,000 volumes) with a copy of the Hebrew writings in Greek. He sent an embassy to the religious authorities in Jerusalem asking for help in carrying out his project, and his request was favorably received. Six men from each of the

71

Twelve Tribes—seventy-two in all—were sent to Egypt, bearing with them a copy of the Law written in letters of gold. According to the legend, the scholars were housed in a monastery on the island of Pharos, and in just seventy days, completed the translation of the Law. By a miracle, all seventy-two independent translations turned out to be word for word the same. The name Septuagint, or LXX (the Roman equivalent for "Seventy") refers to the Greek translation of the Old Testament.

The precious kernel of truth here is that the Old Testament was translated into Greek in Egypt, a land that was neither Greek nor Hebrew. Following in the wake of the invincible Alexander the Great (d. 323 B.C.), a wave of Hellenization swept over the world. Greek became the *lingua franca*, and those who lived far from their homeland soon found themselves speaking Greek. Among them were diaspora Jews in Egypt. Understandably, they wanted to have their own sacred writings available to themselves and their children in the language they read and spoke.

The translation of the Bible into Greek was slow work. It may have begun under Ptolemy, as Aristeas suggests, but a hundred years would elapse before it was finished. Far from being flawless, the translation varied in quality: some of it was very good, and some of it very bad. The Book of Daniel was especially poorly done. But the importance of the LXX can hardly be exaggerated. It was begun and finished by Jews, it was completed by 150 B.C., and the translation was done from a very old Hebrew text, even older than the Hebrew text discovered at Qumran.

The Septuagint, or Greek Old Testament, enabled non-Jews to study the sacred writings of the Jews, and became the official "Bible" of the early Christian Church. It was this Bible that the New Testament quoted so often, and which contained the deuterocanonical books. But of course not everyone liked the LXX, and other versions of the Old Testament appeared: Aquila, Theodotion, and Symmachus among others. It is noteworthy that these last three translations were done between

130 and 200 A.D., by which time polemical sparks were flying between Christians and Jews.

Origen and The *Hexapla*

The LXX suffered much at the hands of its many copiers, and the textual situation was soon a textual mess. Which text was the real LXX? To remedy the confusion, the great Alexandrian scholar, Origen (186-253), nicknamed the Colossus or the Unflappable (*Adamantinus*) by his contemporaries, undertook to produce a Greek version of the Scriptures which would be faithful to the Hebrew text. What he did was to arrange various texts of the Old Testament in six parallel columns, hence the name *Hexapla:*

1	2	3	4	5	6
The Hebrew text	The Hebrew text transliterated in Greek characters	Aquila	Symmachus	Origen's revision of the LXX	Theodotion

Origen's corrected text occupied the fifth column, and so great was his reputation that it was often published alone. Unfortunately he made no attempt to restore the original LXX, but only to "heal" it. He did introduce many changes, but was honest enough to alert his readers of this by a system of diacritical signs.

This giant work—which ran to 50 volumes and 6,500 pages—was the first serious attempt to establish a "critical text." (A critical text is one arrived at by using the principles of textual criticism and accompanied by a "critical apparatus," that is, footnotes referring to sources used and not used. See Chapter Seven.) Origen's critical text was preserved at Caesarea in Palestine, but only fragments of it survived beyond 600 A.D. These the curious reader may contemplate in the pages of Migne's *Patrologia Graeca* (vols. 15-16).

Origen was a great biblical pioneer. Following him there came other men like Eusebius of Caesarea, Lucian, and the Egyptian bishop Hesychius, who brought out their versions of the Greek text. More than a thousand years later, Cardinal Ximenes of Alcala (1437-1517) published an unusual book—the first printed polyglot, containing the text in Hebrew, the LXX, the Vulgate (Latin), T. Onkelos,* and a Greek New Testament. Now available to the modern student is a beautiful Greek edition of the Old Testament edited by A. Rahlfs, Kappler, and Ziegler. It bears the Latin title *Septuaginta,* and was published in Stuttgart in 1935.

Syriac Versions

Many people go through life without ever experiencing the visual pleasure afforded by a Syriac text written in the beautiful script called Estrangelo. The Syriac version of the Old Testament was named the *Peshitta* by Moses b. Kepha (913 A.D.); the word means *simple,* or *common.* The earliest version we know can be dated ca. 464 A.D., but the first Syriac versions must have been done in the first or second century. Some 350 Syrian manuscripts of the New Testament exist today.

Tatian's Diatessaron is a curious work, a Syriac version of all four gospels woven into a continuous narrative. It appears to have been done in Rome toward the end of the second century A.D., ca. 165-180. *Dia-tessaron* means "the Fourfold gospel." The work fell out of favor when Tatian, a disciple of Justin the Martyr (166), became a heretic, and Bishop Theodoret is said to have destroyed 200 copies of it. He did a thorough job, and no complete copy has survived. Much of it can be reconstructed from the commentaries of great Syrians like Ephrem and Aphraates. Fourteen lines of it were discovered in 1933 at Dura Europas, where the first Christian church was built. Apparently

---

*The T. stands for "targum," an edifying Aramaic translation or paraphrase. Onkelos' targum was the most famous of the Palestinian targums. See Chapter Eight.

the Diatessaron was first done in Greek and then translated into Syriac.

Syrcur is the abbreviation for a good Syriac text dating to the second or third century. It was found in 1842 by Mr. W. Cureton, who published it in 1858. It is unusual in that the order of the gospels is: Matthew-Mark-John-Luke. Another interesting manuscript, *Syrsin,* is a palimpsest, a parchment which had been scraped and then written on a second time. *Syrsin* is a text of the Old Syriac gospels, likewise of the second or third century. It was found in 1892 in the Greek monastery at the foot of Mt. Sinai, in St. Catherine's library there, by two enterprising sisters, Mrs. Lewis and Mrs. Gibson, who published it with admirable dispatch in 1894.

The Latin Versions

Old Latin

The term "Old Latin" is applied to all Latin versions of the Bible antedating Jerome's Vulgate. There are 83 texts for the Old Testament and 171 for the New Testament; all are fragmentary and incomplete. The early Christians repeated the actions of the diaspora Jews. The Jews translated their writings from Hebrew into Greek. The Christians had their Scripture translated from Greek into Latin. These translations were carried out as early as the second and as late as the thirteenth century to serve Christians who spoke and read only Latin.

These translations eventually led to the famous Vulgate. In a famous passage, St. Augustine once complained about the bad Latin translations in circulation. "Anyone who thinks he knows Greek and Latin," he wrote, "puts his hand to translating."

By the end of the fourth century, Latin versions of the Scriptures had become very numerous, and presented such conflicting texts that the reigning Pope, St. Damasus (366-384) was moved to remedy the situation. He commissioned the ablest scholar of his day, Hieronymus Stridonensis, known to us as

Jerome, to revise the Latin text in use in the Roman Church. Jerome, born near Venice in what we call Yugoslavia, undertook this arduous and at the time thankless task in 382. Jerome was to be to the West what Origen had been to the East, only with more felicitous results.

The Vulgate

Remarking that there were almost as many versions of the Bible as there were codices, Jerome began by touching up the New Testament. He used the best Greek and Latin texts he could find in Rome, and by 384 had finished the gospels, by 385 a psalter. Exercising great restraint, he found it necessary to make 3,500 changes in the gospels alone, being careful, he said, not to arouse unduly the ire of his critics. He might have saved himself the trouble. So vociferous and vicious were his critics that, shortly after Pope Damasus' death, Jerome found it wise to leave Rome. He went to Bethlehem, established a monastery there, and continued to translate. A rough timetable of his work follows:

382-384 the gospels. Apparently Jerome's New Testament work stopped here.
385   the Roman Psalter
386   the Gallican Psalter
390   Samuel and Kings
392   the minor prophets
394-396 Job, Ezra, Nehemiah, Chronicles, Genesis
398   Proverbs, Song of Songs, Qoheleth (in 3 days) Exodus to Ruth, Esther
404   Judith (one night's work), Tobit (one day's), parts of Daniel.
405   Pentateuch, Joshua, Judges, Ruth
407-418 the major prophets.

Jerome translated most of the Old Testament from the Hebrew; the deuterocanonical books he simply took from the Old

Latin. His New Testament is likewise a combination of both the Old Latin and the Greek manuscripts he found. "We are so far from knowing everything," he wrote, "that it is a lesser fault to say at least something, rather than say nothing at all." He wisely remarked that the aim of a translator ought to be "to reproduce the meaning, not the words, of the original." Jerome was a dedicated and a talented man. His work reflects surprisingly few mistakes, but they are all interesting ones. Occasionally he overemphasized the messianic aspect of some texts. Here are some examples.

Jerome translated Genesis 3:15 as "*ipsa* conteret caput tuum" or "*she* shall crush thy head." The *ipsa* is clearly wrong; the correct word should be *ipsum* (it), referring to the seed of the woman—her offspring. The passage thus means that a particular one of the woman's offspring will crush the head of the devil's offspring. Jerome's mistake is responsible for the many older statues of Mary showing her standing with her foot on the neck of a serpent.

Another interesting slip on Jerome's part occurs in Exodus 34:29. The Vulgate text states that when Moses came down from the mountain, his face was "horned." Thus we have the source for some odd art, especially Michelangelo's famous Moses, complete with horns! Jerome made a mistake. He had read the wrong vowels (e's) into the Hebrew consonants q-r-n giving *qeren* or "horn." Modern translations supply the correct vowels (a's), which change the meaning. Moses' face had become "radiant" as a result of his long conversation with the Lord. This correction was already known in the thirteenth century, and Aquinas remarks that Moses' face was *radiantem, non cornutam* (radiant, not horned).

Even great scholars like Jerome sometimes translate Hebrew when they should not. For example, in one place, Jerome translated the word for the city Ur as "fire." When the word refers to matches (as in modern Hebrew), that is correct. But in Neh 9:7, Jerome has Abraham coming "from the fire of the Chaldeans!" Jerome was doubtless dozing at his seemingly endless task.

How many "gifts of the Holy Spirit?" Six, according to Isaiah, but seven according to Jerome's Isaiah (11:2f). Jerome unaccountably rendered the same Hebrew word *(yir'ath)* in two ways: once (correctly) by *fear of the Lord*, once (incorrectly) by *piety*. This is clearly a case of false piety!

The pre-Vatican II Church used to sing the hymn *Rorate coeli desuper* each year during Advent. It contained one of Jerome's messianic mistakes, for it stated that "the clouds shall rain down the Just One" *(justum)*. The proper translation is "let *justice* descend ... " (Is 45:8).

For Hb 3:18, Jerome has "I will exult in God my Jesus," instead of "in God my Savior."

A verse that is still baffling is Jer 31:22. Jerome rendered it: *femina circumdabit virum*, or "a woman shall encompass (surround) a man." Jerome stressed the messianic possibility a bit too much.

The Vulgate did not meet with instant acclaim, as already noted. However, its intrinsic worth and the sponsorship of Pope Gregory the Great (590-604) enabled it in the end to supersede the Old Latin versions. Modern critics speak of the Vulgate as a notable achievement, a work manifesting both suppleness and versatility and a high quality of exegetical judgment. It is clear, faithful, elegant.*

Jerome's Vulgate has had a long and honorable career in the Church. On April 8, 1546 the Council of Trent declared it an authentic text suitable for public use, thus conferring on it a primacy of place. The Council affirmed its doctrinal, not its critical value. This meant that Christians could rely upon this text because it was free from error in matters of faith and morals. Trent's approval was enough to make the Vulgate the official text for almost 400 years until the appearance of the *Divino Afflante Spiritu* (1943). This encyclical strongly urged Catholic

---

*Many have fallen under Jerome's spell. See E. I. Rand, "St. Jerome the Humanist" in *Founders of the Middle Ages* (Cambridge, Harvard U. Press, 1929); Regine and Madeleine Pernoud's delightful *Saint Jerome* (Macmillan 1962); and J. N. D. Kelly's scholarly *St. Jerome: His Life, Writings, and Controversies* (Harper and Row, 1975).

scholars to turn their attention to translations made directly from the original texts, and not to neglect the study of literary forms.

These recommendations were received eagerly, and in a relatively short time, new and excellent translations began to appear under Catholic auspices. Notable among these are the *Jerusalem Bible* and the *New American Bible* (see pp. 92-93).

As long as manuscripts were copied by hand, the deterioration of texts, including that of Jerome's Vulgate, was inevitable. The progress of decay was momentarily slowed by Charlemagne (742-814), who in 781 commissioned the scholar Alcuin to prepare a revised Bible. In 801, Alcuin presented the desired work to the Emperor. Of this Vulgate, the best representative is Codex Vallicellianus.

Also dating from the time of Charlemagne are some beautiful gospel manuscripts done on white and purple vellum with gold letters. These golden gospels, as they were called, originated in the Rhineland, but they were generally of an inferior quality; the more gold used, it seems, the less exact the text.

In the thirteenth century, France assumed the leadership in biblical studies. A uniform text was established for the use of students at the University of Paris. Under the direction of Stephen Langton, the Paris Bible (1226) was divided into chapters for the first time. While not of a very high standard, the Paris Bibles are important in any history of the Vulgate. The inferior quality of the texts led to collections of corrections, and even the corrections of corrections. The religious orders, especially the Dominicans under Hugh of St. Cher, led the way in compiling such works.

The invention of the printing press stabilized the text by making it possible to reproduce identical texts. John Gutenberg, the inventor of the printing press, was the first man to develop a process successfully combining cheap paper which would take ink, an ink which could be transferred from type to paper, a movable type made of a durable alloy, and a press which insured an even contact between inked type and paper. No other

science began so auspiciously; modern presses are simply re-
finements of Gutenberg's original idea.

Notable Editions

The invention of printing led to a rapid multiplication of critical texts, translations, and versions of the Bible. The first book
ever printed was the Gutenberg Bible (1452-56); it featured the
text of the Paris Bible. It contained 42 lines per page, two columns, 641 leaves. The splendid Mazarin Bible, the first copy of
which was found in 1763 in the library of Cardinal Mazarin
(1602-61), was also a Gutenberg Bible. One of the prize pos-
sessions of the Library of Congress in Washington, D.C. is a
perfect vellum copy of this Bible.

In 1502, work was begun on the Polyglot of Cardinal
Ximenes, or the *Complutensian Polyglot*—a Greek, Latin, and
Hebrew text. Between 1514-17, 600 copies of the Greek Old
Testament appeared; the New Testament followed in 1522.

Desiderius Erasmus (1469-1536), the great Dutch scholar, became the first man to publish a Greek New Testament accompanied by a Latin translation (1516). Yielding to the urgings of
Johannes Froben, a printer in Basle, Erasmus reached the market before Cardinal Ximenes, whose polyglot could not be released until he had returned the manuscripts he had borrowed
to the Vatican. Erasmus consulted only six manuscripts, the
oldest of which was from the tenth century, and his translation
was "precipitated, rather than edited" as he candidly admitted.
Although of no critical value, his translation was an instant success and it was reissued in 1516, 1519, 1522, and 1535. Luther
used Erasmus' second edition when making his own translation.
Erasmus had at first intended to dedicate his work to John
Fisher, then Chancellor at Cambridge. When instead he dedicated it to Pope Leo X, it was drily remarked that he must have
"preferred the Fisherman to the Fisher."

A few decades later Robert Stephen used fifteen additional
manuscripts along with Ximenes' Polyglot in his editions of

1546 and 1549. The third edition (1550) has the distinction of being the first work containing a critical apparatus along with the text, a giant step in biblical scholarship. Another great advance was made in the 1551 edition, when the verses were numbered for the first time.

Theodore Beza, a Swiss scholar and discoverer of Codex D (or Bezae) was responsible for nine editions of the Bible between 1564 and 1605.

Pope Sixtus V issued an authoritative edition of the Vulgate in 1585-1590, based on the eighth century Codex Amiatinus (or A). This edition resembles the text of Stephen, but Sixtus' successor, Pope Clement VIII, replaced it with a revision named the Sixto-Clementine Bible.

The Elzevir Brothers, Bonaventure and Abraham, published a cheap but handy Bible which raced through seven editions from 1624 on. It was a neatly printed Greek text of the New Testament, and was adopted by the British and Foreign Bible Society in 1810. A blurb in the 1633 edition presumptuously stated *Textum ergo habes nunc ab omnibus receptum;* the reader was now in possession of "a text everybody accepted." The reaction was immediate: the "Received Text" was not received by all. Nevertheless the Elzevir Bible was much esteemed and reprinted as late as 1881.

In 1907 the Benedictines of San Girolomo in Rome undertook an exhaustive critical study of Jerome's Vulgate. This seemingly endless task has now been completed. A critical text of the Latin New Testament, complete with apparatus, was begun in 1899 by Wordsworth and completed in 1954 by H. F. D. Sparks.

The English Versions

Translations

The emergence of vernacular versions of the Bible has been a slow and painful process. Latin persisted as the common language in the West until well into the Middle Ages. When the vernacular languages began to develop, the Bible was one of the first books to be translated. This posed a problem, for not every translation was a good one and some of them were simply atrocious. A good, reliable translation was not necessarily the end product of good intentions and diligence. Some translators were poorly prepared; others used their translations as platforms from which to propound their own fiercely held views. Copies even of a good translation were badly made, or tampered with. As we have seen, by the time of St. Jerome the textual situation had become chaotic, and needed the intervention of a pope before it could be restored to a semblance of order.

Here the question of authority emerges once more. On whose authority is one to judge that one translation is a good one and another is not? To a certain extent, the scholars make such judgments. Truth is the daughter of time, not of authority, and the scholars must have their say. But it is also true that the writings gathered together under the title of "Bible" can only be a "Bible" or "Scripture" within the Church. Ultimately there can be no opposition between the Church and Scripture, for it was the Church that "accepted" these writings as expressions of her faith. This view, which some no doubt may find offensive, was clearly stated at Vatican II.

The Bible is of prime importance to the Church. The word of God is the power of God and as such needs no defenders, but as it is handled by men, it needs a Church to watch over it and defend it. Scholars and students of the word are not the only ones who strive to understand the Bible better; this is also the Church's desire as she seeks a more intimate knowledge of God through the sciences and theology. While not telling the scholars their business, she tries to be well informed about their activities as loyal workers within the Church; what they do is certain to have an effect on the body of the faithful.

Early English Versions

Long before the age of printing, men were translating the Bible. Eight manuscripts left by the Saxon invaders of England

THE BIBLE IN ENGLISH

Catholic Versions	Protestant Versions
	1382 Wycliffe
	1525 Tyndale (NT)
	1535 Coverdale (OT/NT)
	1537 Matthew
	1539 The Great Bible
	1539 Taverner
	1557-1560 The Geneva Bible
	1568 The Bishops' Bible
1582 Douay-Rheims (NT)	
1610 Douay-Rheims (OT)	
	1611 King James Bible (AV)
1735 Richard Challoner (NT)	
1750 Challoner (OT)	
1750-78 Challoner Revisions	
	1881-85 Revised Version (RV)
	1901 American Standard Version (ASV)
	1923 The Complete Bible
1937 Spencer (NT)	
1941 Confraternity (NT)	
1944 Knox (OT/NT)	
1952 Confraternity (OT)	
	1952 Revised Standard Version (RSV)
	1960 New American Standard (NASB)
	1961 New World Translation
	1961 New English Bible (NEB)
	1964 The Anchor Bible
1966 Jerusalem Bible (JB)	1966 Good News for Modern Man (NT)
1970 New American Bible (NAB)	1970 NEB complete with Apocrypha
	1971 The Living Bible
	1973 New International Bible (NT)
	1976 Good News for Modern Man (OT)

(449) contain portions of the Scriptures. Others who ventured to render the Bible into English were St. Augustine, the Apostle of Kent (ca. 600), and St. Wilfred (670). Caedmon, a Milton before Milton, sang the story of Genesis, Exodus, and parts of Daniel in verse (ca. 670). St. Bede the Venerable (735), King Alfred (901), and Richard Rolle (1382) also made translations.

These translations were not unusual. Similar efforts to translate the Bible into vernacular languages were made throughout Europe, long before the Protestant Reformation. In Germany, eighteen translations had been made in the fifty-six years before Luther's rendition (1522). Even before the discovery of America, an Italian version (1471), a Dutch (1478), and a French version (1479) had been made. This list, of course, does not pretend to be complete.

In the pages that follow, we shall follow some of the steps, and introduce some of the people, who brought the English Bible down to us.

Violence and passion have been the Bible's companions across the centuries, and this was especially true during the sixteenth century. The seamless robe of Christendom in Europe was sundered at this time—a shattering experience for the common man—and national feelings rose to a fever pitch. Against such a background, the first full-scale English versions of the Bible came into being. For the most part, these translations were done by strong-willed men, sensitive to the excitement of the age and impatient with authority. Violent men, in a violent age—the wonder of it all is that anything beautiful could come out of that seething cauldron. But beauty and strength did emerge from this time.

John Wycliffe (1382)

John Wycliffe (1324-1384), a controversial cleric and priest, was the first man to translate all of the New Testament into English. He was a stormy character, but a pioneer who has left his mark on later ages. His views were carried to fanatical lengths by the Lollards: God must obey the devil, everything is God, brother may marry sister, the papacy is a man-made institution, and transubstantiation is nonsense. A synod held at Blackfriars in 1382 condemned the principal views of the Wycliffites. Interestingly enough, Wycliffe's English Bible was never formally condemned.

William Tyndale (1525)

Tyndale, an ex-Augustinian monk (1484-1536), was the first man to bring out a complete, printed New Testament translated from the Greek. His work was published at Cologne and Worms in Germany, for he had found England ill-disposed to his project. His translation was of lasting value; ninety percent of the Authorized Version (1611) is Tyndale. It was quickly noticed that the new version used the terms "congregation," "overseer," and "elder," instead of "church," "bishop," and "priest." But what brought the wrath of Henry VIII upon the new translation was the arbitrary omission of 1 Pt 2:13-14 ("Submit yourselves to every human institution for the sake of the Lord, whether to the sovereign as supreme, or to the governor as his deputy ..."). Eleven years later, Tyndale was arrested and put to death by the Emperor Charles V, thus becoming a Protestant martyr. Tyndale had defied a Church prohibition against unauthorized translations of the Bible. Many regrets have been expressed that he was put to death for having dared to give Englishmen a Bible in a language they could understand. There is, of course, more to it than that. He omitted a text he did not like, and his enthusiasm for Lutheranism found vigorous expression in the notes accompanying the translation.

The controversy over Tyndale presented Tunstall, the bishop of London, with a painful dilemma: to gather up and destroy a new Bible that crackled with real English idiom, or to ignore it. In the end he chose the first course, and bought up and burned as many copies of Tyndale as he could find. Upon hearing this, Tyndale was delighted, and saw to it that many unsold copies of the 1525 edition were made available to the bishop. He remarked, "I shall thus obtain money to get out of debt, and the

whole world will cry out against the burning of God's word."
He was right about that. Tunstall was a Greek scholar, highly
thought of by his contemporaries, but later writers have de-
plored his action. The execution of Tyndale and the burning of
his Bible remains one of the more painful incidents in the history of the English Church.

Myles Coverdale (1535)

Coverdale (1488-1569) published the first complete English
translation of the Old and New Testaments. He worked from a
Swiss Bible (1529), Luther, Tyndale, and the Vulgate, but not
from the original languages. The deuterocanonical books, along
with 3-4 Esdras and the Prayer of Manasseh, found a place between the two testaments. Coverdale's *Psalter,* loved and sung
for more than 400 years, is the most beautiful of the English
psalters. However, many of Coverdale's notes were polemics
aimed at Roman Catholicism. His language concerning the
Eucharist is shocking and in bad taste. He regarded the Mass as
idolatry, compared the Pope to Caiaphas and Balaam, and attacked confession. The promise of the keys made to Peter alone
(Mt 16:19) is tacitly denied in a title page illustration by picturing all of the Apostles as bearing keys.

Thomas Matthew (1537)

"Thomas Matthew" was a pseudonym for John Rogers
(1509-1555), a follower of Tyndale and an ex-priest. His translation is a compilation of Tyndale (Genesis to Chronicles, and [in
1535] his New Testament) and Coverdale. It is ironic that Tyndale's work, once the object of Henry's anger, was now dedicated to and licensed by him in another form. Matthew added
the Prayer of Manasseh and 3-4 Esdras to the Old Testament.
Many of his notes were indecent and objectionable, being abu-
sive of the Church, her teaching, and her clergy.

Some of the Matthew's translations were occasions of humor
rather than polemics. For example, Matthew's note on 1 Pt 3:7

suggests that if a "wyfe" be not obedient and helpful to him, the husband should endeavor "to beate the feare of God into her heade, that therby she maye be compelled to learne her dutie, and to do it." Matthew's Bible is especially known as The "Bugge" Bible, owing to its rendering of Ps 91:5: "Thou shalt not nede to be afrayed for any bugges* by night." He also quaintly entitled the Song of Songs "The Ballet of Ballettes."

The Great Bible (1539-1541)

A work that exercised enormous influence on England and on all later English versions of the Bible was the Great Bible. It was called by various names: "great" because it measured 9″ by 15″; "Cromwell's," because he participated in its production; and "Cranmer's," because he wrote an Introduction for the second edition. The Great Bible was a combination of Matthew, Tyndale, Erasmus' Latin version, the Polyglot of Ximenes, and the Vulgate.

Copies of the Great Bible were set up in every church, with results that were sometimes deplorable. An authority says that, "The preacher ... often found his exhortations completely drowned out in a tumult of voices, shouting verses of the Bible out loud in various parts of the church, and occasionally adding improvised expositions." One John Porter "with a loud and commanding voice" used to declaim the violent notes found in the Matthew Bible. In the end, the king himself issued an injunction against such interruptions during the celebration of Mass.

The Great Bible contained the deuterocanonical books, and in the prologue to their section, referred to them as *hagiographa,* the term normally used for "sacred writing." Until the appearance of the Bishops' Bible (1568), the Great Bible enjoyed a sort of protected monopoly in the English Church.

---

*"Bugge" meant bogey, or bogey-man—a goblin, bugbear, or specter. The Vulgate had *timore nocturno.*

Taverner's Bible (1539)

Richard Taverner was a lawyer and a scholar, well versed in Greek, less so in Hebrew. He had a remarkable knowledge of the Latin Vulgate as well. By coincidence, his Bible came out in the same year as the Great Bible, which suggests that it might have been a private enterprise. It was, apparently, a polished version of Matthew's Bible, which omitted many of Matthew's offending notes.

The Geneva Bible (1557-60)

After Henry VIII's death, Protestantism triumphed in England under the Protectorate of Edward VI. However, upon the accession of the Catholic Mary Tudor to the throne, the more radical Reformers fled to the Continent and on to Geneva. There, in the home of Calvinism, they met Calvin and Knox, and produced a Bible that was to be known as the Geneva Bible. It at once became popular, and 140 editions were printed up to 1644. The four men involved in its production were William Whittingham, Christopher Goodman, Thomas Sampson, and Richard Cox. Theirs was the most accurate translation up to that time. It also became known as the Breeches Bible because the translators have Adam and Eve making "breeches" for themselves to cover their nakedness (Gn 3:7).

The Geneva New Testament of 1557 was followed by the Old Testament in 1560. The complete Bible met with phenomenal success, and became the "Protestant Family Bible." It is unfortunate that while the text itself had improved, the notes that accompanied it had not. The notes attacked clerical celibacy, the sacraments, the Roman Catholic Church, and the Pope. One can scarcely believe that such abuse was included in the Bible, but this was the mental fare of many sixteenth and seventeenth century Bible readers. It explains to some extent the instinctive hostility some have felt toward the Church of Rome and its leader, the Pope. Such notes are unthinkable today in the

Common Bible which has, since Vatican II, become a happy reality.

The Bishops' Bible (1568)

Tyndale's version had been repeatedly condemned, Coverdale's was not from the original texts, Cranmer's had been condemned by the bishops in 1542, and the Geneva Bible featured a bitter sectarianism. At the instigation of Archbishop Parker, another translation was undertaken and came to be known as the Bishops' Bible because the men involved in it either were or would become bishops. It was of no particular value, however, other than that it was the first text issued on episcopal authority in England, and served as a working basis for the translators of the later Authorized Version.

The Douay-Rheims Bible (1582-1610)

The English Catholic Bible came more slowly than the Protestant versions. It was produced by four men who had been forced to seek refuge on the Continent during Elizabeth's reign. The first of these, William Allen (later a Cardinal), had been in exile since 1561 and had in 1568 opened the English College at Douay, later (1578) moved to Rheims. The priest who carried out the work of translation was Gregory Martin, an Oxford scholar in exile since 1570. Doing two chapters a day, Martin finished the complete Bible by 1582. Two others who assisted in the work of revision were Richard Bristow and William Reynolds. All four men were the pick of Oxford University, and it is to them that we owe the Douay-Rheims Bible.

The Rheims New Testament was published in 1582, but the Old Testament was delayed because of lack of funds. It appeared in 1609-1610, just before the King James Version.

This English Bible was sharply criticized for its literal and antiquated language, and especially for its Latinisms. Much of this criticism is unjust. It was essentially a version of the Vulgate, although the Greek was consulted for the New Testament.

The Vulgate was chosen as a basis of translation instead of Hebrew and Greek for several reasons. Textual criticism as we know it was then non-existent; the collection and collation of manuscripts had only just begun. The Vulgate had also been given primacy of place by the Council of Trent and therefore had authority. Its antiquity was a genuine asset, and it was closer by far to the originals than some of the manuscripts used by the sixteenth century reformers. For all its Latinisms, the Douay-Rheims translation was accurate, and no instances of deliberate perversion or twisting of the text can be shown. And it is not as if Latinisms were everywhere; long passages of the work are not at all unusual in diction. It was, in fact, so good that the translators of the King James Version made extensive use of it.

In the Rhemish version, the notes were at first somewhat caustic. It was not an age to hold back one's feelings, and what Catholic scholar of the time could have resisted a note on Dt 24:1, which described divorce as a thing detestable in the sight of God.

The King James Version (1611)

The King James Version was published in 1611. The Old Testament, except for the Apocrypha, was made from the Hebrew. After 1648 the seven deuterocanonical books were omitted. The New Testament was done from the Greek, but the translators also consulted previous translations, including the Rheims New Testament. The finished product was larger than the Great Bible, being 10½" by 16". As it was appointed to be read in the churches, it came to be known as the *Authorized Version* (AV). It quickly replaced the Bishops' Bible, but victory over the popular Geneva Bible took another fifty years. Once it won that victory, it was not soon again to be seriously challenged.

Remarkably enough, the King James Version was produced by a committee. It has become customary to praise this fine piece of work in superlative terms. It has been called the noblest monument of English prose, and all can admire its simplicity, dignity, and power; its many happy turns of expression and felicities of rhythm; its musical cadences. The King James Version has exercised a lasting influence on English prose, and today, 350 years after its first publication, it is present in homes, hotels, and motels across the country.

At the same time, the King James Version was never perfect, and dissenting voices were quick to make themselves heard. The value of a translation depends largely upon the texts it translates. The Authorized Version did the Old Testament from the Hebrew, but its New Testament derived from the Greek text published by Erasmus—on all counts an inferior text. Yet the Authorized Version became so firmly entrenched that the first serious revision was undertaken 250 years after it was published.

Even the best of authors are at the mercy of typesetters. Moreover, like Homer, scholars occasionally nod at their tasks. Witness the following somewhat amusing examples of mistakes and errors.

The 1631 edition of the Authorized Version astounded its readers by rendering Ex 20:14, "Thou *shalt* commit adultery." Official wrath, at least, was heavy on the printer; such an adulterated text could not be tolerated! Matthew's version had been nicknamed the "Bugge Bible" (because of Ps 91:5), but the Authorized Version earned the title of "The Wicked Bible" for this slip. "The Murderers' Bible" earned its name by its rendition of Mk 7:27: "Let the children first be killed" (for *filled*). There was also a "Wife-Hater Bible," thanks to Lk 14:26: "If a man does not hate his wife ... "; a Vinegar Bible which carried the heading of "Parable of the Vinegar" for Lk 20; and a Place-Makers Bible which had "Blessed are the place-makers" for Mt 5:9. Another amusing misprint has Rebekah and her companions mounting their damsels (for *camels*, Gn 24:61). In one edition Joseph's brothers are described as being the sons of Belial, whereas they were the sons of Bilhah (Gn 37:2). One fears the Midianites who "vex you with their *wives*" (for *wiles*, Nm 25:18). According to 1 Kgs 22:38, "The dogs liked (for *licked*)

Ahab's blood. Ps 119:93 reads: "I shall never forgive (for *forget*) your precepts." More ominously 1 Cor 6:9 reads, in the 1653 edition: "The righteous (this should have been *unrighteous*) shall not possess the kingdom of God."

Recent English Versions

The first serious revision of the Authorized Version was undertaken in the years 1881-1885. A parallel endeavor, taking into account the differences between the English and the American idiom, was the *American Standard Version* (ASV), appearing in 1901. The *Revised Standard Version* (RSV) of 1952 has now largely replaced both the Authorized Version and the American Standard Version. While not a new translation, the RSV has incorporated many of the gains of modern scholarship. This is the version that received an *imprimatur* from Cardinal Cushing of Boston in 1966. It was a complete Bible (the apocrypha were included), and it included no notes of a polemical nature. Endorsed for ecumenical use by individual authorities, the Revised Standard Version (1973) has been given the name of the *Common Bible*.

Among modern Bibles which display a high standard of excellence, the translation put out under the auspices of the Ecole Biblique de Jérusalem stands in a class all by itself. *The Jerusalem Bible* (JB) appeared in French in 1955 and in English in 1966. It was the work of French scholars, including P. de Vaux and P. Benoit, and some fifty others. The enthusiasm which this Bible aroused indicates the high quality of this translation from the original languages. The accompanying notes are strictly directed to the text and contain a mine of information.

The year 1961 marked the appearance of the *New English Bible* (NEB). Undertaken under the auspices of the British Protestant Churches under the direction of Dr. C. H. Dodd, it represents an entirely new, modern translation of the Bible and has been deservedly greeted with enthusiasm. It was the work of many scholars and a panel of literary advisers, and is very readable. Since 1970, the New English Bible has included the Apocrypha.

The *New American Bible* (NAB), published by members of the Catholic Biblical Association, came out in 1970. An impressive contemporary translation, it combines reverence for the text and strict observance of the rules of criticism. Some fifty scholars, all but five of them Catholics, took part in the work.

Modern translations have invaded the paperback market. Special mention may be made of the now complete *Good News for Modern Man* (1966-1976), also known as *Today's English Version*. It features many excellent line drawings illustrating the text, and has received the sponsorship of the American Bible Society. *The Living Bible* (1971) has had an astounding success, and has sold millions of copies. The evangelist Billy Graham has recommended it. It is, however, a deliberate paraphrase and not a translation. Both of these works omit the deuterocanonical books.

J. B. Phillips' *The New Testament in Modern English* (1958) is extremely readable, even lively. Such qualities are unfortunately often achieved at the high cost of making the translation into a paraphrase.

It is always difficult to prophesy, especially about the future. However, it is safe to predict that there will be more translations as each age endeavors to express its knowledge about the Bible in contemporary language. Here, if anywhere, is a field in which one man plows, another plants, another waters, and still another reaps.

Part Two

Understanding the Bible

SIX

HERMENEUTICS: INTERPRETING THE TEXT

What Is Hermeneutics?

The map of a country is not the same as the country itself, and the text of the gospels is not the same as the gospels themselves. It is as important to have good texts of the gospels as it is to have good maps before setting out on a journey. But beyond the maps lies the country to be explored and learned; beyond the text lies a Bible and a gospel to be understood. The hardy traveller has to learn the language of maps. The Christian has to learn how the Bible speaks. Both are confronted by the problem of communication.

Paul assured Timothy that the inspired Scripture was useful on several scores—among which were guiding people's lives and teaching them to be holy. It is *constructive*, in other words. All the more reason for inspecting the foundations, the groundwork, the basic principles required for intelligent interpretation of the Bible's message.

In one sense, the Bible is like those beautiful stretches of countryside that have been the scenes of savage battles. The Bible has always had to make its way amid fierce conflict. No other book has been so criticized, dissected, ridiculed, or praised. It has always had highly articulate critics, and its own magnificent defenders—men like Jerome, Augustine, and P. Lagrange. It lives in an atmosphere of question and debate, simply because it deals with questions that are most important to man—God, man, sin, judgment, salvation.

The eunuch of Queen Candace, while riding back to Egypt after his visit to Jerusalem, found himself having a difficult time understanding Isaiah's mysterious Servant of Yahweh. When the deacon Philip approached his chariot and asked him if he knew what he was reading, the eunuch poignantly replied, "How can I, unless some man show me?" (Acts 8:31).

In the centuries that followed, many men eager to explain the Scriptures came forward, a fact that Jerome found quite irritating:

> Farming, building, carpentry, etc. all require an apprenticeship, but when it comes to interpreting God's word, any gabby old woman, any doddering old fool or dilettante, can blithely dissect it and have a go at explaining it—masters in their ignorance!

Jerome occasionally got off remarks like this, but he had earned his right to an opinion. Readers of the Bible must also earn the right, and part of that healthy pain may be found in the following pages of this book.

Who indeed would not like to spend an hour or two with Philip, or Jerome, or someone else who knows the answers or can point out where and how they can be obtained? Happily, a science exists for exactly that purpose, and Pope Leo XIII referred to it as "the most fruitful part of biblical studies." He was referring of course to what is called *exegesis*—the science of interpretation or explanation.

It is surely wrong to say that biblical interpretation is only for the clergy, historians, linguists, or other experts. One might with equal inaccuracy say that the care of one's health is the concern of one's doctor alone. Using common sense and observing the rules of interpretation, almost anyone can read the Bible with profit.

What is needed is a familiarity with the method of looking at the Bible interpretively. The technical term for this is "hermeneutics." It means looking at the Bible from three different angles: to determine the correct text, to find the ways and means of discovering the meaning of the text, and ways of sharing it with others.

Hermeneutics, a Greek word taken into English, is used in connection with the interpretation of the Bible because Hermes was the messenger of the gods. In a highly stimulating sense, an exegete is the messenger of the most high God. A useful label, hermeneutics is a kind of umbrella under which the sub-branches of the science of interpretation are conveniently gathered. The first branch consists essentially in cataloging the words, the phrases, and the figures used in the Bible. This analysis is not an end in itself but is a means of getting at the author's mind, and at what he meant to say. In academic jargon this is sometimes called *noematics*. University courses in English Literature follow a similar path, when dealing with the classics.

Two thousand years and more of studying the Bible have produced a number of technical tools and rules to help the reader discover the meaning of the Bible text. The second branch of hermeneutics, which concerns itself with these tools and rules, is called *heuristics*.

The third and last branch is, as it were, the calm after the storm, peace after stress. It has to do with getting the finished work of the exegete to the market and into the hands of the reader. In a sense it is both the main course and the dessert. This final branch of hermeneutics is called *prophoristics*.

Fundamentalism

The approach recommended here—the sensitive use of the tools of biblical interpretation—is not taken by all Christians. Many readers of the Bible can be called fundamentalists. They believe that the Bible is completely without error, and that it contains everything the Christian needs to know.

Fundamentalism is actually a subtle and complex position. Here we will say a word about it.

In the world of thought, one powerful movement provokes another. The nineteenth century liberalism, which enthusiastically explained away many long-cherished beliefs under the aegis of common sense and reason, provoked a reaction among conservative Protestant evangelicals that came to be known as fundamentalism. They formed an organization and took their stand on five "fundamentals:" (1) The Bible in its obvious sense is totally inerrant; (2) The divinity of Christ; (3) The virgin birth; (4) The atonement; and (5) The resurrection and future return of Jesus. Fundamentalism also came to be associated with a number of secondary matters—a concern for eschatology and prohibitions on smoking, drinking, and even dancing. These are largely cultural phenomena, tied to a particular time and place, and have little to do with the intellectual position which fundamentalism represents. Here we are discussing the position fundamentalists have taken on the question of the basics of faith.

No one will dispute the importance of basics. A child ignorant of numbers or the alphabet is at a serious disadvantage in school. In like fashion, theologians must have solid principles to work from. "Look to the rock whence you were hewn," was Isaiah's advice (51:1), and Jesus approved the man who built his house upon a rock (Mt 7:24). Is the Bible such a rock?

Fundamentalists say "Yes" to that question. One must believe the Bible from front to back, take it as it is, and not tamper with the text. The Bible says that the world was created in six days, and that Jonah was swallowed by a great fish. These must be true historical facts. The fundamentalist calls for unconditional acceptance of the inerrant Bible as a preliminary step.

In Catholic theology, there can be no room for this sort of fundamentalism. The Bible has always been at home in the Church, and is essential to the Church. But there can be no absolutizing of the material word in which God's message of salvation comes down to us. Literary and historical criticism and the study of literary forms are strongly recommended in Church pronouncements. The main pronouncements on the subject are

Divino Afflante and the 1964 statement of the Pontifical Biblical Commission. At the same time, the same Church body which issued these guidelines also recommends that the faithful nourish themselves at the table of God's word, the Bible.

Now if the Church opposes an exaggerated fundamentalism, she is also opposed to an exaggerated liberalism. Fundamentals are good and necessary, but they need to be carefully formulated. The five classical positions of fundamentalism fail to include such important teachings as the Trinity, the Church, and the sacraments. On the other hand, liberals also go too far in that they become fascinated with their tools, start treating the Bible as a collection of ancient documents, and forget that they are studying a text which speaks of God's plan for man's salvation.

What *is* really basic or essential? The author of Hebrews states that one who comes to God must believe two things: that God is, and that he rewards those who seek Him (Heb 11:6). Aquinas added two other "basics:" the Trinity, and the Incarnation.

Fundamentalism has a powerful appeal and, in fact, is flourishing today as never before. Billy Graham has chosen to be termed a fundamentalist, and he is a potent source of much good through his preaching.

Some current manifestations of fundamentalism are less uplifting. Consider the phenomenal success of books which deal with the end of the world. The authors of such books have combed the book of Revelation (especially chapter 20) for clues to the future, and combine these with the apocalyptic passages from Isaiah, Ezekiel, Daniel, and Zechariah. In the coming battle of Armageddon, the forces of good will clash triumphantly with those of evil. The strategy is mapped out, the battlefield chosen (the Holy Land), and the protagonists are identified (Russia, China, and the West). Signs of the times (wars, famines, cosmic phenomena) are scrutinized and interpreted. The whole is then put together with such precision that the reader can hardly help being caught up in the excitement.

Those who are fascinated with speculations about end times should heed Jesus' words on the subject: "As for the exact day or hour, no one knows it" (Mt 24:36).

"Rational" Exegesis

At the other end of the spectrum is the "rational" approach to the Scriptures, one to which the intellectual current of our age is more sympathetically attuned. Today there are those who consider the remarkable achievements of science as due to the severing of the umbilical cord which bound reason to faith. Immanuel Kant observed in his day that the religion which rashly declared war upon reason would not in the long run prevail against it. But the great thinker Thomas Aquinas considered reason and faith to be complementary wisdoms, not to be sundered; reason was faith's handmaid, not faith's enemy. So it appeared to P. Lagrange, the biblical pioneer who did for modern critical study of the Bible what Thomas Aquinas did for Aristotle: he baptized it, and pressed its positive contributions into the service of the Church—into the service of the Faith. On one memorable occasion Lagrange said: "Let us not attempt to fight against machine guns with crossbows. Let us get some machine guns on our own side." Although not without trial and tribulation, he was successful in doing just that. Under his direction, a galaxy of highly respected scholars manned the ramparts, and their number has grown.

In the remaining pages, reason and faith may be seen as working together in harmony, the one complementing the other in the never-ending task of understanding the word of God. Faith and reason are not two opposed worlds but can aptly be thought of as two concentric circles, the circle of faith embracing the circle of reason.

Literary Forms

The concept of literary forms was first introduced into biblical studies toward the end of the nineteenth century by the German scholar, Overbeck. It has proved to be of significant value.

It begins with a fact: that the form of the writing is an author's way of communicating with his readers. Before he writes, the author selects the form which best sets forth what he wants to say. He can choose prose or poetry. The author can use straightforward prose for narrative, fiction, drama, and history. He can recount a history in the form of annals, saga, epic, folklore, or romance. Biblical writers also used poetry: epic, lyric, didactic, dramatic, prophetic, or apocalyptic in form.

The literary form obviously affects the way we understand the material we read. To grasp the author's meaning, we need to know, for example, whether he is writing straightforward history, lyric poetry (Jos 10:12-13), or apocalyptic prophecy (Dn 9:20-27). Each form has its own rules, style, and conventions. The student of literary forms attempts to apply this knowledge to the Bible and thus understand it more fully.

The great name associated with literary forms is that of H. Gunkel. He suggested that the psalms fell into ·certain categories called *Gattungen*. These categories, he noted, included laments, thanksgivings, messianic and royal psalms, and sheer lyric outpourings of praise. Gunkel went further. He observed that if one studied the *Sitz im Leben* of a psalm—the "real life situation" that had first prompted its writing—one would understand the psalm better. We might also be able to see why the author had chosen that particular literary form.

Here the water deepens quickly. Early in the twentieth century the study of literary forms (which bears in German the formidable name of *Formgeschichtlichemethode)* was applied to the Synoptic Gospels by K. L. Schmidt, M. Dibelius, and R. Bultmann. Vincent Taylor has suggested the following titles for the forms they found there: "Pronouncement and Miracle Stories," "Parables," "Sayings," and "Clusters of Sayings." Instead of studying the *Sitz im Leben,* they studied the *Sitz im Leben Jesu.* The predictable next step was to study the way a particular pericope—a section of a gospel that can stand by itself—was used by the different evangelists. In particular, these critics studied the way certain parables and sayings appeared *in different contexts* in the three gospels. This led them the examine the "editorial process—the *Redaktionsge-schichte*—which helps the reader to perceive the biblical author's particular slant, direction, or purpose in writing.*

The study of literary forms was recommended to Catholic biblical scholars in the *Divino Afflante* (1943). A better appreciation of ancient ways of speaking and writing helps explain many difficulties. But literary forms are neither the last word nor the ultimate consideration of a biblical passage, as a later Church document, the *Dei Verbum* (1965), points out. There are other factors to be taken into consideration, namely those *preliterary* forms of feeling, thinking, and speaking which affected and may even have determined the author's choice of form. These preliterary, and possibly subconscious forms of speech and narration must be given their proper value as expressions of the writer's view of the world and of life. They color his ways of thinking and his value judgments long before he sets pen to paper. Forms of thought and the spirit of a language differ from people to people, from one culture to another, and also from one epoch to another. Yet all of this subtly contributes to the content of the ideas that will be expressed, and to the way in which a message will be understood and received.

The point that has to be stressed is that the Bible cannot always be taken in a strict, literal way. Words are not made of wood, and the Bible cannot be sawed into pieces any more than can our own everyday language. Our ways of communicating with others are extraordinarily supple and diverse. For example, consider the differences among a newspaper's sports pages, a CB radio conversation, and a well-crafted poem skillfully using rhythm and imagery. There are few pleasures in life more satisfying than appreciating the artistry of a well-written story, or a well-told bit of history. The Bible—God's dialogue with his children—contains more than a little bit of all this, and amply repays the knowledgeable reader for his attention.

---

*Note: See R. H. Stein, "What is Redaktionsgeschichte?" in *The Journal of Biblical Literature* 88 (1969), 45ff.

The Bible's Vividness

In his use of the spoken word, Jesus Christ is without an equal. His words, and those of the Bible in general, reach across time and space, and speak to the mind and heart. "No man has ever spoken as this man" was the verdict of his contemporaries.

Mark Twain once remarked that "the difference between the right word and the almost-right word, is the difference between being struck by lightning, or by a lightning-bug." Jesus' words are like that lightning, and apart from a few dreary passages, the rest of the Bible possesses great power as well. The Bible bubbles with the excitement of life and death. Its images are invariably concrete (the Song of Songs, and sections of Ezekiel sometimes too much so), pictorial, startling, clever, moving, surpassingly beautiful. Here are some samples; the reader can find many others.

> Learn a lesson from the way wild flowers grow. They do not work; they do not spin. Yet I assure you, not even Solomon in all his splendor was arrayed like one of these (Mt 6:28f).

> Take my yoke upon your shoulders and learn from me, for I am gentle and humble of heart (11:29).

> Know that the Lord is God;/he made us, his we are;/his people, the flock he tends (Ps 100:3).

> I am like water poured out;/all my bones are racked./My heart has become like wax/melting away within my bosom (22:15).

> I am like a sparrow alone on the housetop (102:8).

> Your piety is like a morning cloud,/like the dew that early passes away (Ho 6:4).

Examples are comparisons, and employ *analogical* language. Two things are juxtaposed (e.g. the mustard seed and the kingdom of Heaven) because they have *something* in common and much that is *not*. What is affirmed, by analogy, is their common aspect or situation. The concept of analogy is an extremely useful one. It enables us to talk about God in human language.

The old Latin proverb "every comparison limps" (*omnis comparatio claudicat*) applies; comparisons do not tell the whole story, and the reader must look beyond them. The great value of comparisons is that they feed the mind, inviting the thinker to see things in another way. They focus the mind on a particular point, providing it with new material, aiding and abetting the understanding.

Parables

Jesus frequently spoke in picture language, and his preaching centered around the kingdom of God. Parable after parable revolved about this theme. Every parable is a simile or comparison drawn out to some length. The kingdom of heaven is "like a man who went out to sow" ... or "like a field oversown with darnel" ... or "like a mustard seed," or "like yeast," "a treasure hidden in a field," "a dragnet." All of the images used were drawn from the life of an ordinary man. Part of Christ's genius was his ability to state a truth in concrete pictures. It was his method of teaching, and he carried the parable to new heights. "No man ever spoke like this man."

Since all of us must take Jesus' teaching to ourselves, it will help to learn a little about how parables work. A parable is a comparison; thus, two elements are involved. Technically these are called the *type*, and the *antitype*. The kingdom of God is the antitype of all the parables—it is the unfamiliar idea. The familiar earthly image is the type or figure. Jesus explained the unfamiliar by comparing it to the familiar. Part of Jesus' genius was the unexpectedness of his comparisons; imagine learning about God's kingdom from a lost coin, or from the seats at a wedding-banquet.

Parables are not elaborations of historical events or real people. Rather, they are stories with a point. A real situation may have served Jesus as a starting point. For example, the publican in the temple, or the scramble for seats at a banquet, may have been incidents which Jesus had actually witnessed. But parables were often imaginary situations, or real situations which Jesus developed with remarkable finesse. The parable of the prodigal son was not a simple tale of a teenager run away from home, but a moral story about the relationship between God and man, elaborated with considerable subtlety. On the other hand, the parable of the wicked husbandmen was clearly drawn from the developing hostility of the Jerusalem authorities toward Jesus.

Jesus did not invent the literary form called parable. The Old Testament contains parables—called *mashal* or *meshalim*—and so does the Talmud. In 2 Sm 12:1-14 is the marvelous parable told by Nathan to David, with a truly magnificent ending— *"Thou* art the man!" Another one is Isaiah's (5:1-7) *mashal* about the vineyard. The purpose of these and similar stories is to bring the reader to concede a point which he may not *at first* understand to be applicable to himself. The story is intriguing in itself. How will it turn out? The reader (or listener) is trapped by his own curiosity. Sometimes an apparently innocent question triggers an answer that is broader or more profound than the questioner had expected. Jesus' parables surpass anything found in the Old Testament or the Talmud, and invariably bear the stamp of brilliance. But they are not always crystal clear. The term *chiaroscura* describes this aspect of parables; they are clear while being obscure, and obscure while being clear. Such a combination of light and shadow is both baffling and stimulating. Just when a reader thinks he has grasped Jesus' point, he begins to notice unsuspected depths in his words, and possibly a personal involvement which he had not bargained for. The gospels record how often those who listened to the carpenter from Nazareth found their minds suddenly racing furiously. Jesus was a good teacher!

Jesus treated many themes in the parables, and by isolating these themes it is possible to see that his teaching revolved around the following points: the approach and arrival of God's kingdom; divine mercy for sinners; the assurance of God's hour (judgment); the need for repentance (personal response); the qualities of a good disciple; the coming Passion and exaltation of the Son of Man; and the consummation (final judgment). (For a discussion, see J. Jeremias, *Parables of Jesus.)*

Parables are essentially comparisons of two elements. To interpret them properly, one has to guard against getting bogged down in details. The rule for interpreting parables is to *look for the main point of the comparison.* How or under what aspect is A (the type) like B (the antitype)? For example, take the parable of the Prodigal Son. A better name for this story would be the parable of the Merciful Father. The main point is the incredible, breathtaking assurance that sinners can count on a welcome in God's kingdom once they turn from their sins, for God is merciful. That is the great lesson of the parable. Over the centuries, Christians have found many other meanings in the details of the parable. However, the main point Jesus wanted to make when he told it is that God is a merciful Father. Parables are not exercises in symbolism or imaginative thinking; they carry within them a central, important point. To discover it, one should compare situation to situation, whole to whole.

Of course, nothing is really simple, at least for long. The gospel parables are not classical stereotypes. Sometimes in the gospel parables are given an interpretation that is *not* according to the rules; that is, sometimes the details *are* exploited, and the parable is treated as if it was an allegory in which everything has a meaning.

Two examples of this procedure are the interpretation of the weeds (Mt 13:36-43) and the fate of the seed (Mk 4:13-20). Jesus himself may have supplied the elaborations; this would simply show that, like any great artist, he was not bound by the rules, but was capable of brilliant variations on a theme. Many reputable scholars, however, among them P. Benoit and Prof. Dodd, see the hand of the primitive Church in these allegorical explanations. Also, in different gospels, some parables are assigned different places in Jesus' preaching, and thus acquire a different emphasis or meaning. This would seem to indicate that the Church adapted Jesus' parables, and even expanded his words, to fit a variety of situations. The themes of Jesus' teaching remain the same, and there is no distorting or changing of his teaching; but the Church, from its experience in preaching the gospel, has on occasion brought out a more explicit meaning of the parables than they may have had in their original form. Commenting on this in his *Dictionary of the Bible,* Fr. McKenzie rightly notes that "one does not recover Christian teaching in a purer and finer form by removing it from its context in the life of the Church."

In this connection, it is again worth drawing attention to Vatican II's profound statement that Bible, Church, and Tradition are truly one, and can never be set off one against the other.

The fact that Jesus so often spoke in parables is puzzling. That he was a man of his times partly explains it, but not completely. If only he had spoken more directly and clearly, we sometimes think. Some have seen in his choice of a veiled form of teaching a certain ambiguity that ill befits the Savior of the world. With 2000 years of Christianity behind us, we find it difficult to grasp the situation Jesus found himself in. His way of indirect teaching was probably the best way he could expound his message without causing riots. Against a background of ancient Jewish monotheism, he could not have uttered two sentences about himself as the true Son of God, God incarnate, without being stoned to death. But if he spoke about yeast and mustard seeds, a prodigal son and a good Samaritan, he realized a twofold purpose: setting forth his message, and gaining time to explain it to those who were well-disposed toward him.

Jesus spoke in parables ("and without parables he did not speak to them"), not out of any desire to be obscure, but rather out of the compassion and mercy which everywhere characterize him in the gospel. This mercy and compassion were combined with infinite love and courage and resourcefulness, and were maintained against all odds even to the bitter end, where they were joined with the forgiveness that he had often advocated and preached.

Metaphors and Allegories

Of all our forms of speech, metaphor is surely one of the most remarkable. It is an ingenious, unexpected combination of ideas, one that delights the mind and the imagination. It calls for a sort of double vision (God is a rock, Herod is a fox), a sensuous image, and a perception of levels of likeness and dissimilarity that we call analogy. Inanimate things find themselves invested with a human personality, with sometimes entrancing results. For example, who is not moved by the psalmist's prayer "Let all the rivers clap their hands, and the mountains shout for joy ... " or his command that "You sun and moon, praise him; praise him, shining stars ... praise him, sea-monsters and all the deeps ... "

Metaphors have the wonderful capacity of translating abstract truths into sensible expression. If a metaphor is sustained and developed, it turns into an allegory (much as simile by its development becomes a parable). No one used it with greater force than Jesus Christ. "I am the vine, you are the branches; my Father is the vinedresser ... " (Jn 15:1-10). Who can forget his words to the disciples: "You are the salt of the earth" (Mt 5:13)? And John the Baptist pointed' to him and said: "Look, there is the Lamb of God!" (Jn 1:29).

On hearing metaphorical language, the mind intuitively grasps the fact that it must not halt at the image. A metaphor stirs the mind; it says something that is both true and not true, yet not wholly untrue either. Herod, able politician that he was,

was a man, not a fox (Lk 13:32). Jesus is not really a vine, except in the sense that he is a source of life to those who are united to him and incorporated into him. Nor was he a woolly lamb, but somehow the image of a lamb, the sacrificial animal par excellence, gentle and innocent of aggression or evil, describes him in a way no other image can.

Metaphorical language, then, suggests more than it actually says. It cannot say everything, and for that reason there are many metaphors, especially when one speaks about God and the mysteries of his kingdom. In a sense, they express something of the inexpressible, and in such a way that the reader subconsciously realizes that there is much more here than what meets the eye or ear.

It is one of the joys of Scripture reading to compile a list of one's own metaphors, to be relished at leisure.

Other Literary Forms

One does not read far in the Scriptures without becoming aware of other forms of expression, many of them still in use today. One of the most frequently used forms is *hyperbole,* a deliberate exaggeration used to heighten the importance of the subject under discussion. Hyperbole abounds in the Old Testament. During the Flood, for example "all the highest mountains everywhere were submerged" (Gn 7:19). Another instance is when Moses led the Israelites from the land of Egypt; in one night, "600,000 men on foot, not counting the children" crossed the waters of the Red Sea (Ex 12:37). During the glorious reign of King Solomon, "silver was as plentiful as stones" (1 Kgs 10:27). St. Paul was using hyperbole when he wrote to remind the Corinthians (1 Cor 4:15) that although they might have "10,000 guardians" in Christ, they had only the one father in the faith, and that was himself.

The Bible also makes generous use of *euphemisms.* This is a way of politely speaking about "unmentionable" things.

Euphemisms are widely used, and indicate a certain level of culture. A euphemism occurs in 1 Sm 24:4, when Saul, hot in pursuit of David, went into a cave "to cover his feet," i.e., to relieve himself. Today we casually refer to restrooms, or powder rooms. Perhaps the greatest of all euphemisms is the reference to death as "sleep" in Jn 11:11: "Lazarus is resting, I am going to wake him." Once again, no one is deceived by this figurative language, and no one takes it literally. It is an accepted way of sensitively communicating certain facts.

Occasionally there is the odd biblical phrase that seems to defy understanding, although to a much lesser extent now that translations aim at rendering ideas instead of mere words. One of the baffling phrases still encountered is that of "a horn of salvation" which God has raised up in the house of his servant David (Lk 1:69). For us, horns are on cars, or are tooted in a band. In a "religious" sense, the *shofar* or ram's horn was blown on a Jewish feast day. All that is wide of the mark, however, for we are dealing here with *metonymy,* according to which a thing is referred to by one particular aspect of the thing. The "thing" here is "the Savior" promised of old to the Chosen People. One of his chief characteristics was to be his "strength;" he would be able to do what he came to do. How to graphically express this to a pastoral or bucolic people? Through the image of the horn, so characteristic of the ram, the leader of the flock, and a sign of his strength, the instrument of his triumph over the foes who attacked the flock.

Another familiar example of metonymy is our customary way of referring to Jesus as "Christ," or "the Christ." He was the "anointed one," the "Messiah." In addition, he is also described by his brilliance and glory; he is to be a "star" rising out of Jacob (Nm 24:17).

A special kind of metonymy, called *synecdoche*, takes a part for the whole, a practice still much in use today. To say "I give you my heart, or my hand," is a way of expressing love or union. Similarly, "the gates" of a city stand for the city itself; he who possesses the one, possesses the other (Jer 14:2).

The one literary form that is rare in the sacred writings is that of *fable*. Fables are not true to life, nor indeed are they possible. In them, animals and trees speak and other impossible things happen. Only two instances of genuine fable occur in the Bible, one where the trees seek a king (Jgs 9:8-15), and another where the thistle (King Amaziah of Judah) spoke to the cedar of Lebanon (King Jehoash of Israel) and was trampled into the ground (2 Kgs 14:9-10). No fables occur in the New Testament.

This concludes our brief survey of the literary resources available to the scribes of Israel. Hopefully it will enable the Bible reader to appreciate the versatility and the skills of the men who helped write the Bible, and will contribute to a better understanding of what they had to say, thus making Bible reading a joy rather than a chore.

Levels of Meaning

The Spiritual Sense

The first thing to look for in the Bible is, of course, its primary or literal meaning. But the Bible is an unusual book full of surprises, and one of these is a special feature not found elsewhere in literature—the spiritual sense. In the past it has been given many names: the typical, prophetical, mystical, or even the allegorical sense (not to be confused with allegory). Since the reader will encounter it in the writings of St. Paul and even on Jesus' lips, it calls for an explanation.

Over and above the literal sense which is found in every single line of the Bible, there seems to be something else—the meaning that is to be found in historical *events*. One such event was the Exodus from Egypt. Under the leadership of Moses, the Israelites went through the waters of the sea, escaping from the harsh slavery of a "pharaoh who knew not Joseph" to emerge into a state of blessed liberty. The Exodus is the historical event in the Bible which foreshadows another deliverance, namely, the liberation of the Christian from the bondage of sin by his passing through the waters of baptism (see Rom 6:3-9) into the freedom of the children of God.

For an authentic spiritual sense, there first must be the type, and the corresponding antitype. Thus for Adam there is Christ; for Melchisedech, Christ again; there is the paschal Lamb, and the manna in the desert, and the molten serpent that was "raised up" (Rom 5:14; Heb 7:1ff; Ex 12:46; Nm 21:6ff). Parallels to these historical events exist in the New Testament. But there can actually be a link between them only if the event is mentioned in the New Testament itself.

The correspondence between the historical event and later reality is an affirmation of the unity and of the continuity of the Old Testament and the New Testament (1 Cor 10:6ff). It is also an argument for the lasting relevance of the Old Testament, as the *Dei Verbum* says. Fanatics like Marcion sought to reject the Old Testament; they met with quick disapproval. In another direction, Origen and the writers of the Alexandrian School went too far in their desire to see spiritual meanings everywhere. Much more reliable is the lowly literal sense, around which alone can a scientific explanation of the sacred text be found.

The Accommodated Sense

What belongs to everybody is bound to be abused and misused, and the Bible is no exception; it has been and is still widely misused and made to say things that never entered the minds of its authors. The chief offenders in this regard are preachers and the writers of pious books. They all too often use the Bible as a springboard into flights of fancy. Half a sentence, even a word or two, are enough to launch whole trains of thought, going off in all directions. A notable offender in this regard was Paul Claudel, a great poet and an ardent believer who found practically everything about mystical theology in the tiny book of Ruth. However inspiring or artistic such works may be, the faithful, as Pius XII said in the *Divino Afflante*, want to know what God has said to us in the sacred writings rather than what an ingenious orator or writer may discover there. What God wished to say is best sought in the literal sense, which keeps its feet on the ground.

A story about the mighty Hercules applies here. While carrying out his onerous tasks, Hercules one day encountered a certain Antaeus, and the two began to fight. The contest went on so long that Hercules began to tire. Antaeus, on the other hand, though repeatedly hurled to the ground, rebounded each time with greater energy than before. Almost at the end of his strength, Hercules began to use his head. Putting two and two together, he reasoned that if Antaeus drew power and vigor from the earth, obviously the thing to do was to keep him from that contact. So Hercules grappled with his foe and held him in the air, off the ground, whereupon he quickly weakened and was destroyed.

The lesson here for the Bible reader is that there is strength—solid ground—in the literal sense and it is to be preferred over other senses. Still, St. Paul himself once made use of the accommodated sense, writing to the Corinthians that they should "not muzzle the ox when it treads out the corn." What he meant was that those who do the work of evangelization should be allowed to share in the goods which their listeners had gathered from their labors.

The Fuller Sense

P. Lagrange once mentioned in passing the possibility of the existence of a "supraliteral sense" over and above the literal and spiritual senses. The expression *sensus plenior* or "fuller sense" was coined by P. Fernandez in the 1920's, and since that time an immense literature has grown up around the subject. It has to do with a strange fact: in various places of the Bible, things are written or said which seem to have a meaning far beyond what the writer or speaker had in mind. Thus, the paschal ritual (Ex 12:46) states that "Not a bone of the lamb should be broken." The Fourth Gospel makes much of this (Jn 19:36), for Jesus' legs were not broken to hasten his death, as were those of the thieves crucified with him. Caiaphas had earlier (11:51) urged Jesus' death as expedient. At this John remarks, "He did not say this on his own. It was rather as high priest for that year that he prophesied that Jesus would die for the nation, and not for the nation only, but to gather together in unity the scattered children of God."

God, author of the Scriptures, is changeless. With the whole of history ever before him, he could see to it that the sacred writers used words which he would later clarify in various ways. Thus in the Bible there are not only passages which the human authors understood and intended; not only correspondences between two concrete, historical realities, one of which signified the other; there is also the fuller sense.

The fuller sense is not found in the mutual opposition of two events, but in the continuity of religious significance between them. It is the enrichment of objective meaning which Old Testament words acquire in New Testament usage. DeVaux calls it a deepening of the literal meaning in a homogeneous way. Being in the text without the knowledge of the author, the fuller sense supposes that value which the text will receive from a later, radically new event—Jesus Christ. It brings out a spiritual value which develops in revelation, reaching its fulfillment in the New Testament. The fuller sense differs from the typical sense in that it has to do with words, not with events.

At the present, the matter of the fuller sense is in a state of rest. Approved by many good scholars, it is not received by others. They argue that the fuller sense can be reduced to the literal (or to the typical) sense, and seems to mean only that the meaning of the whole Bible is greater than that of any single passage in it. At Vatican II, the question was not even brought up.

The following chart may help clarify what is meant by the typical and fuller senses.

Typical: The Sacrifice of Isaac, Abraham's son = Jesus' death
            The manna in the desert = the Eucharist

Typical and Fuller: Isaac, only son = Jesus, *the only-begotten* of the Father
            The Bronze Serpent = Jesus *raised up* on the wood

Fuller: Caiaphas' words = value of Jesus' death for the world
            Gn 1:26: *Let us* make man ... = the Trinity
            Is 6:3: *Holy, holy, holy* ... = God is a triune God.

Heuristics—The Search for Meaning

There is a famous story told about a famous old Greek named Archimedes who, while taking a bath, suddenly solved a difficult problem. He leaped from the tub and, as the story goes, ran through the streets toward the palace, garbed only in a towel, all the while shouting out at the top of his voice: *"Eureka! I have found it."* Archimedes' exultant "Eureka" has the same root as our word *heuristics*. Both mean "I have found it." Heuristics is that branch of hermeneutics which is directed to the search for and discovery of the meaning of the biblical text.

Intelligent reading calls for the observance of certain rules dictated by experience and common sense; as a literary work, the Bible must be read with an eye to those rules. However, since the Bible is not an ordinary book, the ordinary rules will not always suffice. In our discussion of the search for the Bible's meaning, we will first consider some of the rules of literary criticism. Then we will discuss some of the special tools that have been developed for the study of the Bible. Then we will consider the role of the Church in this task of understanding the Bible's meaning.

Rules of Exegesis

The golden rule of exegesis is to find out *what the sacred writer was trying to say* and *what he actually said*. This is the way the interpreter discovers what God wanted to say through the authors' words. The task is not always easy, but neither is it impossible. The first step is to establish the literary form used by the author. The main forms are historical, prophetical, and poetic writing. Each has fairly definite rules.

The interpreter must try to grasp the general cultural conditions of the author's time, since these influence the way the author experienced reality, how he saw things, and why he chose a particular literary form. Gunkel was the first to urge readers to understand the *Sitz im Leben*. Today specialists and other interpreters study all the modes of feeling, speaking, and narration which influenced the author, even before he began to write.

Le style, says the French proverb, *c'est l'homme*. There is much truth in this. A shepherd like Amos, an accountant like Matthew, a cultured man like Isaiah, or a highly educated rabbi like Paul all reveal something of themselves when they write. A Semite's use of bold imagery and his vivid descriptions—along with his habit of bypassing secondary causes and attributing everything to God—can be somewhat disconcerting. So unscientific! And the Semite can talk about God in the most anthropomorphic terms, picturing him as someone walking, molding clay into human shape, breathing. For him God is immanent, yet utterly transcendant. God is everywhere the dominant reality.

Another rule of exegesis is to study the context. All authors risk being quoted out of context and made to say things they never intended to say. If one were to ignore the context, one could justify the most extraordinary things. Isaiah, and Paul, and the writer of Wisdom, can be made to say "Come, let us eat and drink (and be merry), enjoy the good things, and have our fill of costly wine and perfumes (see Is 22:13; 1 Cor 15:32; Wis 2:6f).

Obviously the Bible does not condone the *dolce vita*. Nor did
Jesus condone the sin of adultery when he told the woman
"Neither do I condemn you," for he added "Go, and do not sin
again" (Jn 8:11).

The reader of Scripture must also determine the writer's purpose in writing. Several modern motives for writing—self-
expression and a desire to make money—did not apply at all to
the authors of Scripture. They had a specific purpose, a goal
which they reached through the "sweat and sleepless nights"
which the author of 2 Maccabees complained of (2 Mc 2:26).
This purpose not only sustains an author but influences his
choice and treatment of materials. No two authors ever have
quite the same aim, or display the same nuances of thought and
expression. Even the same author writes for different reasons at
different times. Paul, for example, wrote at various times to
preach, to answer questions, to instruct, to encourage, and to
sometimes scold his readers.

The writers of the gospels similarly differed in their goals.
Mark emphasized the mystery that surrounded Jesus the Messiah, the suffering Son of Man. Matthew was fascinated by
Jesus' words; he grouped them together and emphasized them
even in the narrative sections of his gospel. A disciplined man,
Matthew also had a catechetical purpose. He presented Jesus'
teachings not in a mechanical fashion, but in a way that reflected the experience which the early Church had of the person and meaning of Jesus. On the other hand, Luke was concerned with the marvelous fact that salvation was not just for the
Chosen People but for all mankind. His gospel begins and ends
in Jerusalem. John seems to have had another purpose: to interpret the significance of the gospel. His view of Jesus includes
everything the synoptics said of him, but more. John views
Jesus as the incarnate Word of God, the Son from all eternity
who became man to share his divinity with men. The believer
here and now possesses the divine life that is the goal of salvation. In sharing in the life of the Father, Son, and Holy Spirit,
the believer will live the same life he now lives in the Church,

whose sacramental "signs" point to that divine life.

The purpose, context, and intention of any author demand the close attention of any reader. By being alert to these rules, we can come even closer to an understanding of Scripture. Any close study of this kind will eventually require the reader to seek help from those who have gone before him. The reader of the Bible has at his disposal a vast array of specialized tools—ranging from highly technical studies to popularizations of scholarship. It is time to examine these "tools of the trade."

Aids to Scripture Study

Concordances

At the most basic level are concordances—dictionaries which list every word in the Bible, except for prepositions and pronouns and the like. Concordances are often very useful. They allow the reader to quickly locate any desired text simply by looking up a pertinent word in the text. For example, where did Jesus say, "I am the vine?" Under the word *vine* are listed all the places in the Bible where that word appears, beginning with Genesis and on through the Bible to the end of the New Testament. With a concordance, one can trace the use and development of certain ideas throughout the Bible.

The first concordance was one on "morals" and was compiled by St. Anthony of Padua (1231). In 1244, Hugh of St. Cher drew up the first complete biblical concordance, and a similar concordance was published in 1470, shortly after the invention of printing. A concordance for the Hebrew Bible was completed by 1448, but not printed until 1523. In 1550, John Marbeck drew up the first English concordance; another, dating to 1737 and often reprinted, is the famous Crudens concordance to the King James Version. A Vulgate concordance, by Thompson-Stock, appeared in 1947. Young's *Analytical Concordance* came out in 1965. A totally new kind of work in this genre is the 1976 *Modern Concordance to the New Testament*, a highly sophisti-

cated and handsomely presented work edited by Sr. Jeanne
D'Arc, O.P. It contains listings under 341 themes, informs the
reader which Greek word has been used, and serves the King
James, Revised Standard Version, Jerusalem Bible, New Ameri-
can Bible, New English Bible, and The Living Bible. *Nelson's
Complete Concordance of the New American Bible,* edited by
Fr. Stephen Hartdegen, O.F.M., made its welcome appearance
in 1977.

Synopses and Harmonies

The student of the New Testament often wishes to study how
the writers of the gospels treat the same event. A synopsis aids
in this by presenting the synoptic gospels—Matthew, Mark, and
Luke—in parallel columns. The arrangement makes comparison
easy and saves much time for the scholar. Larfeld's *Griechische
Synopse* (1911) indicates in boldface letters where the synoptic
gospels agree in the choice of words (and even the roots of the
verbs), and where they disagree. A good, modern Greek example is the *Synopse der drei ersten Evangelien* (Huck-Lietzmann,
1936). This is now available in English under the title *Gospel
Parallels* (1961), using the Revised Standard Version text (1952).

When the text of the Fourth Gospel is printed on one page in
parallel columns with the three synoptics, we have what is
called a harmony. Fr. Stephen Hartdegen's *Chronological
Harmony of the Gospels* (1942) used the revised text of the
Challoner-Rheims version, and followed pretty much the order
of M. J. Lagrange's *Greek Synopsis Evangelica* (1926). A recent
variation now on the market is R. J. Swanson's *Horizontal
Synopsis of the Gospels* (1975). It presents the Revised
Standard Version texts for all four gospels one under the other,
an arrangement that brings out the similarities and dissimilarities clearly.

Geographical Atlases

Recently there have appeared many excellent atlases of the
Bible, complete with illustrations, photographs, and maps, all

accompanied by explanatory texts. Few of these can match the *Atlas of the Bible* put out in 1956 by L. H. Grollenberg. This first-rate work by an alumnus of the Ecole Biblique de Jérusalem was translated from the French by J. Reid and H. H. Rowley. Also available and helpful are D. Baly's *Geographical Companion to the Bible* (1963) and the revised edition of *The Westminster Historical Atlas to the Bible* (1956), edited by G. Ernest Wright and F. V. Filson. The *Macmillan Bible Atlas* (1975) deserves special mention for its attractive disposition of texts and maps.

Suggestions for Your Library

For those who read only English there are many good books to consult, some of them written by lifelong students of the Bible, others by teams of scholars. Well worth acquiring is B. W. Anderson's *Understanding the Old Testament* (1975). P. de Vaux's *Ancient Israel* (1961) is something of a classic, but for most a book to be dipped into on occasion. Three books that are valuable additions to one's library are J. L. McKenzie's *Dictionary of the Bible* (1965), the *Jerusalem Bible* (1966), and the *Jerome Biblical Commentary* (1968). The *Jerusalem Bible* with its extensive notes (found only in the big edition), and the *Jerome Biblical Commentary* with its commentary on all the books of the Bible and its valuable background articles, are extremely useful tools. They may put a crimp in one's budget, but are good lifetime investments.

Abbreviations

The reader of scholarly works on the Bible may be momentarily confused by different styles of abbreviations for the books of the Bible. Abbreviations for the books of the Bible are listed in the front of most modern Bibles. Those in the *Jerusalem Bible* are very short; all but ten of the books are referred to by two letters, and sometimes by one (examples: Gn, Ex, Dt, 1 K, 1 M). The *New English Bible* uses three and sometimes four letters (Gen, Exod, Deut, 1 Kgs), and the *New American Bible* strikes a middle course (Gn, Ex, Dt, 1 Kgs, 1 Mc). This book uses the *New American Bible* style. All of these styles are quickly mastered, and save both time and space. Various other abbreviations can be taken in stride.

Occasionally, the abbreviation *l.p.* or *loc. par.* may crop up in the margins of some Bibles. This stands for "parallel places," and means that the reader should look to see how the other evangelists treated the same subject. A synopsis does this for the reader, but not everybody has such a book.

To give an example showing the value of the *loc. par.* let us take the word *almah*. In Gn 24:43 it is used of Rebecca; in Ex 2:8 it is applied to Moses' sister Mary; in the Song of Songs 6:8 it refers to the young maidens. It is not surprising, then, that the translators of the LXX rendered *almah* by *parthenos*, or *virgin* (Is 7:14). Usage within the Bible seems to justify the translation, although of late some versions (JB, NEB) use *maiden* or *young woman*. The NAB, however, sticks with the word *virgin*, and has an excellent note on the matter.

Dictionaries

An excellent *Greek-English Lexicon of the New Testament,* by Arndt-Gingrich, is at the disposal of students who know some Greek. It is a gift offered to the English-speaking world by the Lutheran Church, Missiouri Synod (1957). A *Concise Greek-English Dictionary of the New Testament* (1971) is tied to the United Bible Societies' *Greek New Testament*. Much more ambitious is G. Kittel's *Theological Dictionary of the New Testament* (1965-1974), which contains an article on every theological term used in the New Testament. It is very detailed and must be used with caution, since some of the articles are slanted.

In this context, mention should be made of James Barr's excellent *Semantics of Biblical Language* (1961). Just having a good dictionary is not enough; languages change, and idiomatic expressions convey special meanings. For example, in Ps 95:11 we read: "I swore in my anger, if they would reach the place of rest."

The Hebrew use of "if" here is equivalent to a negation—"They shall *not* enter into my rest" (so JB, NEB, NAB). Another example is Paul's word, *apolutrosis*. In ordinary Greek, it meant the liberation of a slave by purchase, but on Paul's lips it signified another kind of liberation entirely—the redemption of the believer from the slavery of sin.

Of course these suggestions are not intended to be exclusive or final. Of the making of books, especially books on the Bible, there is no end.

The Role of the Church in Interpretation

It is not always easy, despite the most exhaustive research, to grasp just what the sacred writers were trying to say. The Bible contains many enigmas and unsuspected depths, whether the research is done by Church scholars or by those without any denominational affiliation. These labors often shed much light upon the Bible, but not infrequently they reveal the limited vision of the scholars. The fact that even the professionals disagree often among themselves is an indication that they have not attained to the real meaning of the Scriptures.

Scholars even disagree on how much they themselves can be trusted. The eminent J. Jeremias conceded that scholarly exegetes have made mistakes, but felt that ever-more-exact methods would give ever-greater protection against these in the future. He thought that if we make ourselves dependent upon exegesis, we need not fear that we are setting about a dangerous undertaking to which there may be no end. At this, the equally respected Käseman exploded: "On the contrary, it seems to me safer to walk through a minefield blindfolded! . . . Is it possible for us to forget for a second that we are daily concerned with a flood of doubtful, even abstruse ideas, in the field of exegesis, history, and theology, and that our scholarship has gradually deteriorated into a worldwide guerilla warfare . . . ?"*

For Catholics, the ultimate interpretation of the Bible rests

Exegetische Versuche und Besinnungen, II (1964), p. 36f; quoted in *Commentary on the Documents of Vatican II* (1968) p. 193.

with the teaching Church. Still, as the recent *Dei Verbum* makes clear, the Church does not dictate to scholars what they are to do or how they are to do it, but simply reminds them that the Church is deeply interested in their work precisely because it concerns the Bible. The insistence of the early Reformers that Scripture alone was enough would have astounded the early Christians. Cardinal Newman wrote that since the inspired word is but a dead letter (ordinarily considered) except as transmitted from one mind to another, there is always the need for a living teacher. Newman thought that this teacher was the Church. This, in essence, is the Catholic position on interpretation. The process whereby Christian doctrine has been handed down from one generation to another goes all the way back to the primitive Church. The Church is the place par excellence where Scripture is heard in its fullest and truest meaning. Church, Bible, and Tradition cannot be pitted one against the other; they rise or fall together. The work of the exegetes is part of the Church's endeavor to understand God's word; it is their noble privilege to help "mature" the judgment of the Church.

The Church's position on biblical interpretation does not imply a rejection of proper exegetical method. True piety cannot spurn scholarly technique. On the other hand, piety is not the slave of technique. The search for meaning in the Bible may begin with the findings of critical historical research but it does not end there. When the good of the whole believing community requires it, the teaching Church is divinely guided to express the true meaning both of the Bible and of the doctrines of the Church.

It is interesting to realize that the Church has officially spoken about the Bible fewer than twenty times. Considering the size and importance of the Bible, this is a remarkable fact. Never once has the Church intervened to settle questions of a historical or scientific nature, not even in the painful case of Galileo. And even in these few cases of authoritative definition, some feel that the Church was using Scripture only to illustrate its stand, and was not "defining" the literal sense of those passages.

The Fathers of the Church

The Church's involvement in biblical interpretation extends to and rests upon the early Fathers of the Church. These vigorous, articulate, and courageous defenders of the faith appeared on the scene as the apostolic preachers died. Their era extended from 150 to 600 A. D. Their writings fill many volumes, first assembled in Abbé Migne's *Patrologia Graeca ... et Latina,* and now in many modern vernacular editions.

A Father of the Church was a Christian known for his holiness (this excludes Origen), for his orthodoxy (this rules out Tertullian), and by the fact that he was recognized as a Father of the Church by the Church which he served.

The importance of the Fathers lies in this: they were living links in the chain of tradition; they were vital parts of the process by which the mystery of Jesus Christ was understood, developed, and handed on to later generations. Already aware of tradition—their acceptance of the canon indicates this—they were themselves a part of that tradition, speaking for the faith in Rome, Alexandria, Antioch, and other great cities of the ancient world. Their lifespans so overlap that during this period the Church never lacked great champions, and the Bible was never without great expositors.

What is unique about the Fathers is that, unlike the great uncial manuscripts, they at least can be precisely located in time. This means that in their writings we encounter biblical texts which are older than the oldest extant manuscripts. For example, the Vaticanus codex is of the fourth century, but Justin died in 164, Irenaeus died in 202, and Clement of Alexandria in 215. Only the papyri which are now coming to light contain older New Testament texts than their writings do. True, the Fathers' quotations of Scripture were sometimes from memory, or were mere allusions to the texts, but their antiquity lends them special importance.

Modern biblical scholars are invited to consult the Fathers as theologians, not as museum pieces. The methods and results of modern interpretation often differ widely from those of the Fathers, but there is still that area of theological insight which is of great importance. Rash indeed would be the exegete who would contradict the unanimous teaching of the Fathers. Such unanimity does exist in many pivotal places: the Incarnation, Trinity, and divinity of Jesus Christ. As might be expected, some of the Fathers were ordinary men, but some of them—Jerome and Augustine—were giants of Church history. The student of the Bible should read their biographies in the *New Catholic Encyclopedia* to understand their importance and the influence they exercised upon the whole Church.

Some of the Fathers were also called Doctors of the Church. The original four were Ambrose, Augustine, Jerome, and Gregory the Great. Pope St. Pius V added Thomas Aquinas from the Western Church and four more from the Eastern Church: John Chrysostom, Basil the Great, Gregory Nazianzen, and Athanasius.

The Pontifical Commission for Biblical Studies

In this century, the Catholic Church has exercised much of its responsibility for biblical interpretation through the Pontifical Commission for Biblical Studies. The role of the commission has changed over the years, and the story reveals much about how the Church views the Bible.

The Biblical Commission was set up in Rome in 1903 as a clearinghouse for special biblical problems. It was an arm of the Pope, headed by a cardinal and composed of consultors—experts in biblical and oriental matters. Questions addressed to the Holy See concerning the Bible were referred to them. It was the commission's responsibility to provide suitable guidelines for the handling of such difficulties. The commission was established at a time when the Church, emerging from the tumultuous nineteenth century, was mainly concerned to survive at all. The comission at first exhibited a guarded and very conservative attitude toward the new learning. The replies from the Biblical

Commission, officially termed "responses" or "declarations" (but not decrees), did little to spark pioneer work among Church scholars.

There were then, to be sure, exceptions: innovative and realistic scholars continued to be open to the new knowledge. To their great credit, they persisted heroically in trying to gain a hearing for what was good in the new trends, while remaining loyal to the Church.

From 1905 to 1915, the Biblical Commission issued a series of responses to fourteen queries about the Old and New Testaments. Few responses appeared in the next twenty-five years, but then, while P. Jacques Vosté, O. P. was Secretary of the Commission, the *Divino Afflante Spiritu* burst like a beneficent bombshell upon the Catholic world. The Pope's encyclical changed the Church's stance. It looked with favor on modern methods of biblical study and encouraged Catholic scholars to employ these methods in their work. P. Vosté and his successor, P. Athanasius Miller, implemented the encyclical. P. Miller wrote "The [biblical] research worker can obviously continue his investigations with complete freedom." A heady breath of fresh air began to blow through the field of Catholic biblical studies as the encyclical took hold. P. Vosté had written that the earlier answers of the Biblical Commission, concerning Genesis, were actually quite elastic and needed no further elaboration. P. Miller assured Catholic scholars that they were under no obligation to follow the previous directives. P. Vosté had discussed the literary forms found in Gn 1-11; P. Miller reminded interpreters that they were to exercise their liberty in a responsible fashion. In the aftermath of such statements, Roman Catholic biblical scholarship has blossomed.

Is the Biblical Commission an organ of censorship which restricts truth? Not at all. Authoritative guidance serves to protect the "little ones of God's flock" and also safeguards the public from wild and irresponsible scholarship. Not everyone can or should cope with the complicated problems of exegesis which lie close to the heart of the traditional faith. Notwithstanding these reflections, some will always resent any kind of discipline, and others will fear new ideas. The Biblical Commission represents a prudent middle way, described by the poet Alexander Pope:

> Be not the first by whom the new are tried
> Nor yet the last to lay the old aside.

Far from seeking to maintain the status quo against desperate odds, the Biblical Commission shows itself to be alert and well informed, and able to profit by modern scholarship. Witness the contribution it made during the course of Vatican II by its "Instruction on the Historical Truth of the Gospels." This far-reaching document contributed much to the final form of the *Constitution on Divine Revelation* (the *Dei Verbum*), and is another welcome indication of the Church's ability to consult with experts, listen to them, and assimilate the truth with divine wisdom.

How then does one go about the business of discovering the meaning of the Scriptures? First, by paying close attention to what the authors were trying to say, by being conscious of the context in which they spoke, and by appreciating the aims and objectives which lay behind and colored what they actually said.

In addition, one should always read the Bible theologically, which simply means that we should not interpret the Bible against the Bible, or against the faith, or in ignorance of tradition, or in any arbitrary and willful fashion.

Prophoristics–Presenting the Message

Faith comes by hearing, as St. Paul says, and by the grace of God. St. Augustine, a great lover of the Bible, must have had this in mind when he observed:

> "The man who is supported by, and holds firmly to, faith, hope and charity, has no need of the Scriptures, unless he is to instruct others. Many people live by these three virtues in the desert, without books."

Augustine, of course, wrote these words long before John Gutenberg invented the printing press. The situation has changed greatly from Augustine's day to the present. The Bible is now available to all Christians, and all Christians should read it. Nevertheless, it is true that salvation does not depend on a man's ability to read or write, however much such skills enrich a man's life and his faith.

Modern Translations

The hunger man feels for the word of God is insatiable, and believers have tried, in a wide variety of circumstances, to keep in touch with that word. In prison camps and behind the Iron Curtain, the Bible brings with it light and consolation and the knowledge of God's loving plan of salvation. There is strength to be gained from the Bible, even by touching, kissing, and seeing it raised to positions of honor. There is something here that appeals to man's deepest yearnings.

The best way to spread knowledge of God's word is through modern vernacular versions of the Bible. One cannot but applaud the efforts of those who thus bring to a wide public the work of biblical experts, historians, archaeologists, and theologians. The Bible is now available in 1600 different languages, and the presses are never still. Only the very young will not remember how far we have come, and how quickly!

In Chapter five we mentioned English versions old and new, paying special attention to the *Jerusalem Bible,* the *New American Bible,* and the *New English Bible* (see pp. 92-93). Each of these translations contains improvements in text and language that make Bible reading a pleasure. There will be other new translations, for new evidence keeps coming in, and our speech patterns constantly change. There is always room for new translations; like children, each one has something the others do not.

Paraphrases

A paraphrase differs from a translation in that it is aimed, as were the ancient Jewish targums, at helping the reader understand what is being said to him. The Bible was not written for scholars alone, but for all. Paraphrases do not cling tightly to the words or word-order of the text. Sometimes they are elaborations of the text, as Ronald Knox's *New Testament* and *Psalms* (and *Old Testament,* for that matter) often were. There is no denying that Knox often reads more entertainingly than some translations which follow the Bible's text scrupulously. *The Living Bible* also makes for lively reading,* but one has the uneasy feeling that the text is being lost in the enjoyment of it. In paraphrases, difficult passages tend to be made clearer than they actually are, and there is always the possibility that the paraphraser is being carried away by his enthusiasms or prejudices in interpretation. In the end it is always the text, and the intention of the author of that text, that count. They are to be respected even when they are obscure.

Commentaries

The Bible exercises an extraordinary fascination over the minds of men, and as a result there are many biblical journals catering to a wide variety of readers, treating at various levels points of history, archaeology, and non-biblical parallels which impinge upon the Bible story. *The Bible Today* contains articles on biblical topics on a popular level; the *Catholic Biblical Quarterly* and the *Journal of Biblical Literature* provide a forum for scholarly reports of progress in research.

There are also books which deal with the text of the bible itself, and they are called *commentaries.* Here too there is a great variety. Some commentaries are popular, as is the Collegeville *Old and New Testament Reading Guides.* Others are fearfully erudite as are *International Critical Commentary* and the *Etudes Bibliques.* The *Anchor Bible* is one of the latest ventures in this field, and the contributors are both Catholic and Protestant. A recent and well-written popular commentary is the *Tyn-*

---

*The Good Samaritan leaves "a couple of twenties" with the innkeeper; and Jesus calls Peter "Rocky."

dale Commentary on the New Testament (ed. R.V.G. Tasker) available in paperback (20 vols).

In some commentaries, a gospel is explained pericope by pericope; the text is sometimes supplied, sometimes not, for reasons of economy. In others, the text may be deployed across the top of the page, Greek or Hebrew on the left, translation on the right; commentary is made verse by verse below. In the *Jerome Biblical Commentary* and *Peake's Commentary on the Bible*, there is no text at all, but simply chapter and verse numbers, and a word or two of the text with explanations following.

The ideal commentary is not one where the author uses the Bible to present his pet theories, or to slay his pet dragons. The text and its message are the important things and the commentator should stick to them. The ideal commentary should moreover aim at the reader's heart as well as at his mind, for the Bible is a religious book and deserves both theological and practical treatment. There is no reason why a commentary cannot serve both to illumine the mind and to nourish the reader's faith. God's people hunger for such spiritual food. Some commentaries, alas, instead of turning water into wine, turn the wine into water!

It is of course too much to look for a perfect commentary. Scholars write mostly for scholars, and popularizers skim off only the cream. These approaches are far from perfect, but there is room for both. A good rule of thumb is to enjoy the light where one finds it, not always expecting to be bathed and warmed by it. Life gives nothing to mortals, as Horace said, without great effort on their part, and Thomas Aquinas noted dryly that it is better to achieve some good, however imperfect, than never to make a mistake.

One could hardly find a better justification for the writing of even an imperfect commentary, or these pages of background to the Bible.

SEVEN

LOWER CRITICISM: TOWARD AN ACCURATE TEXT

Today's motorists speed along superhighways and thread their way smoothly along the orderly lanes of busy city streets. They take for granted the careful planning and hard work that made such travel possible. In a similiar fashion, readers of the Bible take the existence of vernacular versions for granted. How these came to be is not their concern, but it is very much the concern of scholars who are known as textual critics.

It should be interesting and instructive to take a quick look at these little-known men to see how they work, for they are the engineers of our modern biblical texts. Their work leads to "changes" in the text, changes resented by some, and welcomed by others. Their work is aimed at the refinement and improvement of biblical texts.

Textual criticism is both an art and a science. More specifically it is a part of a science called Lower Criticism. It is concerned with determining the accuracy of the text through study of ancient manuscripts of the Bible. The interpretation of the text is not its primary goal; that belongs to another group of scholars whose business is Higher Criticism, or hermeneutics.

The textual critic operates in a theatre of complexity and confusion of such colossal proportions as to strike dismay into all but the strongest of hearts. Basically, this is the situation: for the New Testament alone, there are some 5000 handwritten manuscripts. Some of these are complete but many are fragmentary. Roughly, there are 2500 uncials, 2600 minuscules, 81 officially recognized papyri, and 1997 lectionaries or books containing passages from the New Testament that were used in the liturgy. No two of these manuscripts are exactly alike. In fact, there are more variant readings than there are words in the original text! It is the task of the textual critic to work his way backwards through this forest of manuscripts and their next-to-infinite variations in order to establish the oldest and the most reliable text. In other words, he is trying to restore the original text from which these ancient manuscripts were drawn.

The originals of all the books of the Bible have long ago perished, not from neglect, but because the original materials have simply disintegrated or been destroyed during times of persecution. This of course poses a problem. How can we be sure that our modern text corresponds to the original text? J. A. T. Robinson in his fascinating paperback, *Can We Trust The New Testament?* puts the matter graphically: How can we be sure that the train entering the tunnel—a period of time extending from 30 A.D. to 250 A.D.—is the same train that comes out of the tunnel? In other words, has the teaching of Jesus, or that of the apostles, been changed during the two hundred and more years that elapsed between Jesus and our most ancient manuscript evidence for his teaching?

As a matter of fact, we are able to reproduce or reconstruct these manuscripts with a high degree of accuracy. There is an abundance of evidence to work with. The number of available New Testament manuscripts is far greater than exists for any other work of ancient literature. For Sophocles, for example, there are one hundred extant manuscripts; for Aeschylus, fifty; for Catullus, three; for Tacitus' *Annals,* one. By contrast, for the New Testament there are, besides the 5000 Greek manuscripts mentioned above, 8000 Latin, and 1000 in other languages. Moreover, our manuscripts stand much closer to the original writing than is the case with almost any other piece of ancient literature. The oldest manuscript of Plato (d. 347 B.C.) dates from 895 A.D., a gap of over a thousand years. For Vergil the gap is 300 years. The gap for the New Testament is well under 300 years.

Thus we are surprisingly close to the original gospel. The chances of any notable wide-scale corruption of the text in transmission are small indeed. And the train that comes out of the tunnel is the one that went into it.

Systems of Reference

The textual critic's first job is to catalogue the thousands of manuscripts with which he must deal. There are now three systems of references in use, all of them German in origin.

1. Johann Wettstein (1693-1754) was the first man to adopt John Mill's (1645-1707) suggestion that uncials be assigned boldface capital letters, and minuscules given simple numbers. It was not a bad idea as long as there were only a handful of manuscripts to deal with. Soon it became necessary to borrow Greek letters, and in the nineteenth century, the Hebrew letter *aleph* was used for the C. Sinaiticus manuscript (**S** was also used).

2. As new manuscripts continued to turn up, Philadelphia-born Caspar Gregory (1846-1917) next proposed that all uncials be indicated by an **O** followed by a number (both boldface); the lower the number, the older the manuscript. Simple numbers identified the minuscules. The Greek papyri discovered in the eighteenth century were listed with a boldface Old German **P** plus a number, e.g., **P**66. This is a practical system; the numbers can go on indefintely. In 1969 for example, 300 new New Testament texts were added to the list. However, this system's weakness was that it referred only to the type of manuscript. This led to the formulation of a third system.

3. Objecting to a code that merely told the reader what *kind* of writing he might expect in a manuscript, Hermann von Soden (1852-1914) proposed a way of letting the reader know what he would find *in* a given manuscript. Each manuscript was given a number; the lower the number, the older the manuscript. Pre-

ceding each number, however, was a lower-case Greek letter describing the contents. Thus dl (the "d" is for *diatheke*, or *testament*) was a text containing the whole of the New Testament. Or, a1001 ("a" is for *apostolos*) is one in which the gospels were missing (and sometimes Revelation); or e55 (the "e" is for *euangellion*) signified that the text contained only the gospels.

Von Soden's system was so complicated that it never gained wide acceptance. However, modern lists of manuscripts utilize his "d," "e," and "a," and have added to them the letter "c" (for the catholic or non-Pauline epistles) and an "r" (for Revelation).

The Names of Manuscripts

The stock in trade of the textual critic is, of course, the manuscripts of the Bible. Some of these are things of beauty; all of them are unique productions and each one is different. Pictures of the famous codices reveal that each one has its own singular personality. Some are exquisitely written (Vaticanus, for example); others are scrawly and unattractive. There are manuscripts of one, two, three, and even four columns. The names of manuscripts come from different sources. Some tell of their place of discovery; for example, Codex (or C.) Sinaiticus was found in the Monastery of St. Catherine at the foot of Mt. Sinai by Tischendorf in 1844. Other names tell of the place of origin. For example, C. Alexandrinus was probably written in Alexandria in Egypt. Some names indicate where a manuscript is to be found. C. Vaticanus is in the Vatican Library in Rome; it has been there since 1475, before Columbus discovered America. A manuscript may bear a name that describes it. Thus, C. Ephraemi Rescriptus is a *palimpsest,* a parchment where a second text has been written over a first which has been erased as well as possible. With the help of sophisticated modern photographic techniques it is sometimes possible to retrieve the separate texts. Finally, a manuscript is sometimes named after its owner. Thus, C. Bezae was so called because it was obtained by Theodore Beza, Calvin's friend. Beza presented the manuscript to

Cambridge in 1581, whence its other name C. Bezae Cantabrigiensis.

Some Famous Manuscripts

Vaticanus (**B** or **03** or d1) dates from the first half of the fourth century. This beautiful uncial measures 10″ by 10½″, and has three columns per page. Of the original 820 pages, 759 have survived. It is not known how it reached the Vatican Library, where it was first listed in 1475. It contains all of the Old Testament and the New Testament to Heb 9:14.

Sinaiticus (**S** or **01** or d2), almost as old as Vaticanus, measures 15″ by 13½″ and has four columns per page. It contains almost all of the New Testament. Of 730 pages, 347 remain. The story of its discovery by Tischendorf is a fascinating one (see Finegan, *Light from the Ancient Past* and Metzger, *Text of the New Testament).* Since 1933, the manuscript has been in the British Museum. Like Vaticanus, it is written in a beautiful script.

Alexandrinus (**A** or **02** or d4) contains the whole Bible written in two columns. A date of ca 450 is given to it. It has 773 of its original 820 pages, and includes two letters of Clement of Rome. The codex came to England in 1628 and has been in the British Museum since 1751. The manuscript is quite large, measuring 12⅝″ by 10⅜″.

Ephraemi Rescriptus (**C** or **04** or d3). Housed now in the National Library in Paris, this one-column manuscript is the most important palimpsest of the New Testament. Some 200 pages long, it contains an ancient fifth century text over which was written (at right angles) a Greek version of Ephrem the Syrian's treatises.

Washingtonenis (**W** or **032** or eO14, is a fifth century text containing all four gospels: Matthew, John, Luke, Mark.

Bezae (**D** or **05** or d5), a sixth century manuscript with 406 of its original 510 pages remaining. The gospels and Acts are in both Greek and Latin, and it is the oldest bilingual manuscript extant. In it the gospels are arranged in apostolic order: Matthew, John, Luke, Mark.

Claromontanus (**D** or **06** or a1026) is a Greek-Latin manuscript contemporary with C. Bezae and of the mid-sixth century. It has thirteen Pauline epistles.

With few exceptions the minuscules are of little value to the textual critic, since they are for the most part recent manuscripts, dating from the ninth century on. However, some minuscules are copies of ancient majuscules now lost, and for that reason they represent a very old text.

It is customary to refer to the minuscules by italicized Arabic numerals, *1, 2, 3*, etc. This differentiates them from the uncials (which are identified by boldface capital letters) and from the Latin manuscripts (indicated by lowercase italicized letters of the alphabet).

There are very many minuscules, as has been noted. They too can be grouped into families which have a common source. Thus Family 1, containing a third-fourth century text, is grouped with 118, 131, and 209; it is given a special symbol (f1) for identification. The Ferrar Group, or Family 13, dates from the eleventh century, but represents a much earlier text. It is interesting to note that in this group, the pericope of the woman taken in adultery comes after Lk 21:38, i.e. immediately before the Last Supper. Another minuscule, 1739, derives from a fourth century text and contains the Pauline epistles.

Reading Footnotes

Armed with this information, the reader may now pick up a critical text constructed according to the principles of textual criticism and be able to cope with its critical apparatus, or footnotes. The apparatus contains the authorities behind the editor's choice of text, and show that he is aware of the options. The uncials are referred to singly (**A, B, C**) or in families (**H** for the Hesychian or Egyptian readings; **K** for the Koine text). The minuscules appear: *1, 2, 3*, etc. So do the Latin manuscripts:

singly—*a*, *b*, *c*, and collectively: *OL* for Old Latin, *vg* for Vulgate, *it* for the Itala. Where the papyri are cited, one notes **P66** and **P75**. Ancient lectionaries are indicated by an italicized letter *l*, followed by a number, e.g., *l*60. The Fathers are listed by abbreviated names: Or(igen), Ambr(osius), Athan(asius), Aug(ustinus), etc.

Scattered liberally throughout the text and margins are what are called diacritical marks, signs, and numbers, all of which remind the reader of variations or omissions occurring in other manuscripts.

Not everything that can be found in the footnotes is of earth-shaking importance, but everything there testifies to the careful work of the scholars who are trying to establish the original texts of the Scriptures. Modern editions of critical Greek and other texts explain these footnotes in lengthy introductions. Nestle's *Novum Testamentum Graece* does this in four languages: German, English, Latin, and Swedish.

Textual Criticism in Action

It is time now to see how the textual critic goes about his work. He must, first of all, be competent in Hebrew and Greek, must know the materials (papyri, uncials, minuscules, lectionaries and ancient versions), must be acquainted with the writings of the Fathers, and in addition, be blessed with patience, persistence, good eyesight, and sound judgment. Such a man assumes the tremendous task of finding the correct reading of any given text. There are so many variants, or variant readings, that one thinks of the needle in the haystack. For example, is the name *Asaph*, or *Asa?* Should the text read *Christ Jesus*, or *Jesus Christ*, or simply *Christ?* Jesus went *with the Twelve*, or was it with his *twelve disciples?* Did he take *a* cup, or *the* cup? Should the text read, *See where he* or *where the Lord*, was laid?

The reader may be saying to himself, What difference does it make? The sense is there. Why quibble about such minutiae? The answer, of course, is that only one of the readings is correct, and often variants make a difference in the sense of a passage. So the textual critic patiently sifts through the variants—some of them unintentional and some of them deliberate—to see which is the correct reading. There is a saying in French à propos here, that a good carpenter cannot pray well on a prie-dieu that rocks.

Unintentional errors are usually easy to spot. For example, in one manuscript of Acts 19:34, *dittography* occurs: "Great is Diana of the Ephesians of the Ephesians." Elsewhere we find the opposite, *haplography* or writing a letter once when it should be written twice. In Lk 10:32, some manuscripts have *praso* for *prasso*. There are times when the copyist skipped a line, because when he looked back at the text to find the word he had just copied, he would pick up the same word but farther on. Omissions caused this way are called *parablepsis* or *homoioteleuton*. Then too, due to poor eyesight, the copyist would sometimes mistake letters like OC (hos=*who*) for *theos* (*God*).

Another hazard of the professional scribe was hearing. The ancient monks often copied under dictation, and would put down the wrong letters. Certain vowels and combinations of vowels (*ei e oi i ui u* and *eta*) were all pronounced *ee*. Thus *humos* (you) became *hemos* (we). The two Greek o's, omicron and omega, also gave the scribes trouble. *Exŏmen* (we have) thus became *exōmen* (let us have). *Ek sou* (out of you) became *eks ou* (whence). No doubt the copyists also lost their concentration on occasion, and this led to a change in the order of the words, or the unconscious use of synonyms. The imperfect form *eipe* (he said) easily slid into the aorist *ephe* (he said);* and sometimes an *ek* replaced an *apo*. There were unconscious errors of judgments also. A scribe might wrongly copy a marginal gloss, thinking it to be part of the text. In this respect, the worst manuscript of all is the fourteenth century minuscule 109,

---

*The imperfect tense of the verb indicates that the "action" was repeated in the past; the aorist, that it took place once.

whose copyist copied the genealogy of Jesus straight across two pages. The results were simply fascinating: everyone has the wrong father and God himself becomes the son of Aram!

Intentional changes also occurred. Some of these involved faulty spelling and grammar, obvious mistakes which are easily corrected. More serious were the harmonizing tendencies which caused the infiltration of verses from one gospel into another. Thus Luke's *Our Father* is filled out so that it matches Matthew's. Luke's title on the Cross (23:38) is made to correspond to Jn 19:20 "written Hebrew, Latin, and Greek." Additions also can be found: Jesus came not merely to call sinners, but to call them "to penance" (Mt 9:13). Paul is not only a "minister" or "deacon," but also "an apostle and a herald" (Col 1:23). Sometimes historical or geographical difficulties are clarified. For example, Mk 1:2 contains quotes from Mal 3:1 and Is 40:3, but Mark credits Isaiah alone. A scribe tried to clear this up by making the text read: "written in the prophets." Origen's changing of "Bethania" to "Bethabara" is well known (Jn 1:28). Elsewhere, scribes would fuse variant readings. In this fashion, Acts 20:28 became, "the church *of the Lord and of God.*"

Finally, there are deliberate doctrinal alterations. The heretic Marcion was a pioneer in making the sacred text support his private teachings, but Christians were in their turn sometimes guilty of bending the text a bit, or omitting phrases thought to be too harsh, or superfluous, or difficult to reconcile with accepted teaching. Here are some examples. Jesus' statement (Mk 13:32) that he did not know when the day of the Lord would come, is simply dropped from some texts. Jesus' "father and mother"(Lk 2:33) becomes "Joseph and his [Jesus'] mother" in many manuscripts. The word "parents" (Lk 2:41, 43, 48) is in some cases changed to "Joseph and Mary" or simply omitted. One final example. To avoid classifying Jesus with two "other" criminals (Lk 23:32), some scribes changed the sequence of the words.

For the most part, however, the ancient copiers of manuscripts were careful and painstaking workmen. Many of them faithfully copied out difficult readings, resisting the temptation to correct them. For example, scribes copying Gal 2:12 faithfully wrote *elthen* even though the sense of the passage calls for a plural *(elthon)*. Copyists of Phil 2:1 wrote *ei tis* (whoever), although *ei ti* (whatever) is preferable.

The regularity of the script and the disposition of the texts sometimes border on true beauty, but all the manuscripts are monuments to the faith that prompted them to be written and thus preserved. There is no calculating the dedication and training which produced these ancient manuscripts which speak to us across the ages about the wonderful things of God.

Rules for the Textual Critic

The New Testament comes down to us across fourteen centuries of handwritten manuscripts, no two of which are in total agreement. To discover the original readings out of thousands of variants may appear to be a hopeless task, but a number of good rules have been worked out to protect the critic from arbitrary decisions. These *modi procedendi* were formulated by Griesbach (1745-1812) and have since been refined. The reader may find himself surprised at them, for they are really principles of intrinsic possibility and in fact some of them are downright clever.

The first rule is this: if a reading is to have any value at all, it *must have appeared in some ancient source* like **B, S, A, C,** or the papyri. Thus the date and character of the witness must be taken into account. The second rule is that the critic should observe the *geographical distribution of the sources* that support a variant. If a variant, for example, appears in Antioch, Alexandria, and Gaul—widely separated and independent—it has a good chance of being the genuine text.

Pausing for a moment, let us have an example of what the critic does. The ending of the Our Father (Mt 6:13) has often puzzled Bible readers. Are we to ask for deliverance from *evil* or from *the Evil One?* The Greek text cannot answer that; it can be either, grammatically speaking. But how shocking! The

Lord's Prayer ending with the word *evil*, or *devil?* Someone may have thought this improper, and so appended a pious doxology: "For thine is the kingdom, and the power, and the glory." Much better! Yet, demurs the textual critic, that is not a reading found in **S B D** *or f*1, nor in the earliest commentators (Tertullian, Origen, etc.), nor precisely like that in the Didache, or Old Syrian, or Old Latin. It may have come from 1 Chr 29:11-13, or have been a liturgical adaptation (Chrysostom's?), but it is not the original reading.

The third rule is: *the shorter reading is more probably the correct reading.* The temptation to fill out, to expand, or to clarify the text was a constant one, and quite marked in some manuscripts. But the rule must be carefully applied, inasmuch as the shorter reading may make no sense at all, because something essential has been omitted due to some momentary inattention on the part of the scribe. However, there are times when it applies. The famous *Johannine comma,* a clause inserted in 1 Jn 5:7-8, is clearly an addition. Only four Greek manuscripts, all of them late, have the text. None of the Greek Fathers, even those involved in the Trinitarian controversies, ever used it. Moreover, if it was original, it is impossible to explain its absence in practically all the manuscripts.

Another example where the shorter text is clearly the better is the pericope of the woman taken in adultery (Jn 7:53-8:11). Textually, no case can be made out for it as a genuine Johannine text; it simply lacks satisfactory credentials. Yet the pericope is a piece of oral tradition, known even before St. Jerome, and is to be considered as both historical and inspired. It has appeared after Lk 21:38, incidentally, in *f*13. In this case, then, the shorter text, Jn 7:52 followed by 8:12, is the correct one.

According to the fourth rule, *the more difficult reading has a good chance of being the right one.* This is a fairly good rule of thumb. The difficulty referred to is not the modern reader's, but that of the ancient scribe copying out a text. When he came upon a text that seemed to him less natural or difficult to understand, he would sometimes solve the difficulty by changing the text. It is of course obvious that no scribe in his right mind (barring involuntary lapses or accidents) would take a text that was clear and make it obscure. The reverse, however, might easily be the case.

To illustrate: in Mk 15:34, Jesus cried out on the cross, *Eloi, Eloi ... !* The majority of the uncials and minuscules have this reading, but Codex Bezae and Koridethi have, instead, *Elei, Elei ... !* Which is correct? Aside from the strong numerical support for *Eloi,* (manuscripts are to be weighed, not counted), *Eloi* is the more difficult reading. In the sentence that follows, the bystanders mock Jesus, taking up his words in derision: *Eli*-ahu he calls on ... ! If Jesus had said *Eloi,* why would the crowd have come back with *Eli(ahu)?* Their reaction, however, would be understandable if he had originally said *Eli, Eli ...* Thus, a few copyists made the more difficult reading into an easy one. But the preferred reading will be the one that is difficult.

For the textual critic, the fifth rule is the golden rule: *Find the text which best accounts for the rise of the other variant readings,* or the one that best fits the author's writing habits, or what the author was more likely to have written.

The textual critic is a man who works in those delicate areas where one must be aware of nuances of meaning. He must be able to discern various degrees of probability. The rules of textual criticism are good as far as they go, but they are by no means to be applied in a mechanical or rigid way. Problems cannot be solved simply by counting noses either. Biblical manuscripts, like people, have definite characteristics or personalities, and their strengths and weaknesses have always to be taken into consideration. One good manuscript may outweigh any number of inferior witnesses. A later manuscript may be preferable to older ones if it is a copy of an older text. The United Bible Society's Bible indicates by footnotes—A, B, C, or D—the degree of probability accorded to particular readings.

The work of textual criticism continues. It is never simply an intellectual game, although it requires much intelligence. It is a necessary means of understanding the Scriptures with its message of salvation.

A Short History of Textual Criticism

Textual criticism began in earnest after the invention of printing, and its history falls into three rather well-defined periods.

From Cardinal Ximenes to the Elzevir Brothers

The pioneer of modern textual criticism is Cardinal Ximenes, the compiler of the Complutensian Polyglot (1514-1522). Next came the famous humanist Desiderius Erasmus, who in great, if not unseemly, haste consulted only six manuscripts and produced the first printed Greek-Latin New Testament. The novelty of his work offset its many defects, and it quickly ran through six editions (1516-1551). The famous printer, Robert Estienne or Stephen, consulted fifteen manuscripts, introducing verse numbers in the 1551 edition. Stephen's text was close to that of Erasmus, as were the nine editions put out by Theodore Beza (1564). The next noteworthy accomplishment was the publication of a small and handy New Testament by the two Dutch brothers, Bonaventure and Abraham Elzevir (1624-1633); it too was based on the texts of Stephen and Beza. A publisher's blurb informed the reader: "Now you have a text that is received by everybody." The work was in fact warmly received, and for the next 200 years was the standard text. The publisher, however, had overstated the case: the *textus receptus* was not received by everybody, for it became increasingly clear that it had been based upon relatively few and definitely inferior manuscripts from which no really good translation could be made. Ironically it was the *textus receptus* that served as a basis for the King James Version and for all the early English translations of the New Testament.

The Golden Age of the *Textus Receptus*

The long life of the *textus receptus* (1633-1831) was due in large part to the scarcity of manuscript witnesses to a better text.

It is interesting to note that the C. Alexandrinus came to England in 1628, that C. Vaticanus was first seen by Richard Bentley in 1720. But the C. Sinaiticus was discovered only in 1844 and the oldest papyri (52, 60, and 66) have been known only from 1935-1960. Lacking such important materials, the early textual critics found the going against the firmly entrenched *textus receptus* rather difficult. But even without the great uncials and the papyri, they kept making out a case for a better text. Variant readings began to be shown: B. Walton introduced those from C. Alexandrinus (1657); J. Mill, the true father of modern textual criticism, printed (1707) Stephen's 1550 edition together with some 30,000 variant readings taken from A, D, and other manuscripts.

About this time, Richard Simon (1638-1712), a Roman Catholic and author of an epochal critical edition of the New Testament (1678), saw his work of biblical criticism set at naught by the opposition of the great Bossuet. Many at this time held that if the New Testament contained so many variants, the text was hopelessly uncertain. Others with equal vehemence held that it was time to stop all critical tampering with the sacred text. Both positions were brilliantly rejected by Richard Bentley (1662-1742). Following him, J. A. Bengel (1687-1752) argued that one should weigh the evidence and not simply count the witnesses. He also introduced the idea of the "difficult reading" as a rule of thumb in deciding which reading was better. Bengel also suggested the notion that manuscripts belonged to groups or families (which he named Asiatic and African). This last idea would be developed by Semler (1725-1791) and Griesbach (1745-1812) into a threefold grouping: Western, Alexandrian, and Byzantine families. With his fifteen rules for textual criticism, Griesbach put textual criticism on a truly scientific basis. In 1808, another Roman Catholic scholar, J. L. Hug (1765-1846), suggested that the oldest of our uncials were in fact revisions of a second century text: one by Origen, in Palestine; a second by Hesychius, in Egypt; and a third in Antioch by Lucian.

From this brief survey of the heyday of the *textus receptus*, it is evident how great the work of textual criticism is, and how significant the contributions of the scholars just mentioned. At the end of this period, J. M. A. Scholz (1794-1852) published a two-volume New Testament, using 616 new manuscripts, while also providing the first comprehensive listing of the Greek manuscripts of the New Testament available at that time (1830-1836).

The New Age of Textual Criticism

A definite break with the *textus receptus* was first made in K. Lachmann's Greek New Testament in 1831. Lachmann (1793-1851) was followed by the impressive Lobegott Friedrich Constantin Tischendorf (1815-1874), the discoverer of C. Sinaiticus and of eighteen other uncials and six minuscules. He also edited for the first time or made new editions of many other manuscripts, among them Sinaiticus and Vaticanus. He was "the man with the apparatus," and his *Editio octava critica maior* of the New Testament (1869-1872) contained some 3500 changes in the text, all buttressed by evidence from the manuscripts, versions, and the Fathers. The *textus receptus* was now left far behind.

The *New Testament in the Original Greek*, published in 1881, was the work of two Cambridge professors, B. F. Westcott (1825-1901) and F. J. A. Hort (1828-1892). Their preference was clearly for B, S, A, but especially B. Vaticanus was also favored by B. Weiss in his Greek New Testament (1894-1900). R. Weymouth took ten different editions into account and his work, *The Resultant Greek Testament* (1886, 1892, and 1905) was a synthesis of previous critical works. Vaticanus was also much esteemed by E. Nestle (1851-1913). His *Novum Testamentum Graece* (1901) went through many editions (the 25th in 1963!) and has for all practical purposes become the new *textus receptus*.

The last great collection of manuscripts was effected by P. Lagrange (1855-1938) in his *Introduction à l'étude du Nou-*

veau Testament (1933-37). In this work he argues that three or four recensions occurred before our manuscripts attained their present shape. Manuscripts were like people, he said, with definite personalities or types. Their age was important, but the pro's and con's of a manuscript have to be weighed, and in the end one may follow a good manuscript even if others disagree. If positive doubt remains, it can be pointed out in the apparatus. Still, manuscripts bear family characteristics, and modern textual criticism has been able to sort out four different types of texts: (1) the Popular or Western; (2) The Alexandrian; (3) The Byzantine (or Syrian); and (4) The Caesarean. Lagrange called this last the "nerve-center of all New Testament criticism." The best manuscripts belong to the Alexandrian and Caesarean families.

The work of textual criticism is never ending. In 1967, a project was begun to produce a *Novi Testamenti Graeci Editio Maior,* a new critical Greek text of the New Testament. It will incorporate all available evidence to date—a formidable but necessary undertaking—and it involves scholars from seven European institutes and schools, and from the Ecole Biblique in Jerusalem.

EIGHT

THE BIBLICAL LANGUAGES

The original books of the Bible were written in different languages. Most of the Old Testament was written in Hebrew; a few books were composed in Greek, and there are a few Aramaic passages. All of the New Testament was written in Greek, although there is an ancient opinion that Matthew was first done in Aramaic. Jesus and his disciples spoke Aramaic, but probably could get along in Greek as well. Greek at that time was, like English today, an international language.

Charles Peguy once lamented his ignorance of the Hebrew language, for that meant he could not comprehend the Bible as a Hebrew reader might. He was partly right but not completely. A knowledge of Hebrew will not automatically enable a modern reader to understand the Hebrew mentality and grasp the subtle allusions of the mother tongue. At the same time, we can learn much about the Hebrew mind by reading those scholars and interpreters who know Hebrew well. In this matter, where men share a common Bible, and where each man is at the service of all believers, one can sense a host of believers of every age, peering over his shoulders and reading the words with him.

Hebrew

Biblical Hebrew is a flectional tongue belonging to a group of Northwest Semitic languages (See chart). Semitic languages read from right to left and for many centuries were written without vowels. In Indo-European languages—the family of languages which includes Greek, Latin, and English—the writing is from left to right, and the consonants are always accompanied by vowels.

Since the sixth century A.D. Hebrew has been written with the vowels underneath or occasionally over the consonants. Most of the Hebrew letters are formed by using parts of a square. It has four gutturals, and it is hard for native English-speakers to produce the proper sound of two of them—*ayin* and *heth*. Another odd feature of Hebrew concerns verbs. The simple form of the verb is the third person singular, and usually is made up of three letters. The verb is conjugated by adding on to the front or the back or to both ends of the root. There are verb forms referring to masculine or feminine: *kathav* = "he writes",

COMMON SEMITIC LANGUAGES

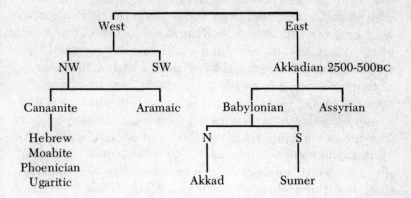

INDO-EUROPEAN

Greek
Latin
Slavic
Russian

kathavah = "she writes", etc. As for time-forms, Hebrew has only a perfect tense used for the present, and an imperfect which serves as *both* imperfect and future. This double use of the imperfect causes difficulties for translators: were the prophets referring to the past or the future?

Hebrew has no adjectives as we understand them. The phrase "a golden mountain" is written "a mountain of gold." Structurally, the language is inferior to Greek and is not a good vehicle for abstract thought. There are no subordinate clauses. Almost everything can be and usually is introduced by "and." For example, the Book of Exodus begins "And these are the names ..." In such cases translators can ignore the "and."

Hebrew was spoken from the time of Abraham until after the Babylonian Captivity (587-538 B.C.), when it yielded to the more supple Aramaic. Today, after a long rest, Hebrew is enjoying a second life as a living language: it is the official tongue of the State of Israel.

Despite its drawbacks, the Hebrew language can be highly praised and appreciated even by non-linguists. It is a concrete language, very direct and sometimes earthy. The very poverty of the language—its relatively small vocabulary—means that some words have layers and layers of meaning. A good example of this is the word *hesed*, long translated "loving-kindness" or "steadfast love." Actually *hesed* is a covenant word, implying a relationship that is more personal than legal, a bond of loyalty. The Jerusalem Bible translates the word as "tenderness;" it is all that, and more (see Hos 2:21; 4:2; 6:6). Another good example is the word "knowledge." To us knowledge means information, but the Hebrew knowledge of God was "covenant-oriented"—a "knowledge" of the heart. The Hebrew "knows" God as he "knows" his wife—with a deep personal understanding and love. Still another word would be *anawim* or "the poor." This term goes beyond material poverty to mean also those whose whole life and future are in God's hands.

The reader of the Bible can, without even learning to read the

Hebrew alphabet, gradually build up for himself a little fund of information about Hebrew which will give him some security and satisfaction in reading the Bible. Just to know, for example, that a Hebrew word ending in *-im* or *-oth* is a plural form (m. and f.) is illuminating. A reference to *targumim* or *bamoth* makes a bit more sense. Then there is the *kosher basar* on the windows of Jewish meat markets. *Kosher* means legal; *kosher basar* means meat that has been butchered in accordance with the Law: "Flesh with its lifeblood still in it you shall not eat . . . Make sure that you do not partake of the blood, for blood is life" (Gn 9:4; Dt 12:23). When a man loses enough blood, he weakens and dies; there is a mysterious connection between the two. In the eyes of every Hebrew, life was a gift from God that was to be respected, along with the blood of which it is a sign. This avoidance of contact with the blood persists to this day.

God gave life, the Bible relates, by breathing into man's nostrils, and the man became a "living being," a *nepeš hayyah.* *Nepeš* (pronounced *nefesh*), is not the soul as opposed to the body, but a breath, a living principle, a man's very self, his person, or what we might call his Ego. The very name for man, in Hebrew, defines him as one who lives by the breath of God.

To illustrate the importance Semitic peoples attach to names, I would like to share with the reader an experience I once had atop the Herodion, the cone-shaped hill one can see from Bethlehem when he looks toward the Dead Sea. I was standing there one day when a very cheerful, ragged, and colorful boy seemed to suddenly materialize before my eyes. Naturally I took a picture of him. He then asked me to give him the photo. With many gestures and halting Arabic I explained that it would take a few days to develop and print the film, but that I would be happy to send him a copy. Reaching into my pocket for a pencil and paper, I then asked, *Shu ismak*—"What is your name?" To my astonishment he backed away, obviously uneasy, and indicated that he was not interested in the picture after all.

He would not give me his name, for my having it in writing and in my pocket might signify that I owned him, or had some power over him.

There are biblical reverberations to this story. When Adam named the animals, the meaning is not that he presided over some gigantic, prehistoric circus parade, calling one animal a giraffe, another a hippopotamus, etc. The point was that the man (Adam) was superior to all the animals, and had the power to name them. The name *is* the thing named, and describes the thing.

The Bible contains many illustrations of the importance of names. God changed Abram's name to Abraham. Adam gave Eve her name. Nebuchadnezzar changed Mattaniah's name to Zedekiah and made him king (2 Kgs 24:17). Pharaoh Neco made Eliakim king, but imposed a new name upon him—Jehoiakim. In this way vassal kings were made to understand just where they stood.

The Hebrews manifested a special reverence for the divine name *Yahweh*, which they would never pronounce. Instead, whenever they encountered it in their reading, they substituted for it the name *Adonai (adon* means *noble lord)*. In the centuries that followed, the vowels from this word Adonai were applied, with proper phonetic changes called for by the letters themselves and by the accent, to the four letters of the divine name (YHWH is called the "sacred tetragrammaton"). And thus the non-word "Jehovah" was born. Not a Hebrew word at all, it was first coined in the thirteenth century A.D.*

There are many names for God. In the Bible, El, Elohim, and Yahweh are of prime importance. Many people in the Bible bear theophoric names, which contain a part of the divine name. For example: Daniel is Dani + El; Elizabeth is Eli + zabeth). Some names end in *iah*, an abbreviation from Yahweh. Thus Isaiah, Jeremiah, etc. It might be useful to point out that modern English Bibles have adopted this Hebrew spelling; the

---

*A Jew attending Hebrew classes at the Ecole Biblique when I was there used to read *hash-shem* (which means "the name") when he came to YHWH.

Greek forms, Isaias, Jeremias, etc. have been dropped.

The word *Messiah* is not theophoric, but comes from the Hebrew word for "anointed." Translated into Greek, Messiah became *Christos.* Thus Christ is not Jesus' second name, or surname, but rather a descriptive title. Jesus means Savior; Jesus Christ means Anointed Savior.

The Jewish word *shema* means "Listen!" The Shema is the Jewish Credo or profession of faith, and comes from Dt 6:4-9; Ex 20:2-17. (See Dt 11:13-21; Nm 15:37-41.) Even today, devout Jews often nail a little container called a *mezuzah* on their doorframes. Inside the mezuzah, miniaturized and printed on a tightly rolled slip of paper, are the Ten Commandments and the Shema, which goes like this: "Hear, O Israel! The Lord is our God, the Lord alone! ... You shall love the Lord, your God, with all your heart, and with all your soul, and with all your strength." As a devout Jew goes in and out of his house, he touches the mezuzah, much as devout Catholics used to bless themselves with holy water. These words made a deep impression upon Jesus, and his *new* commandment echoes the Shema: "You shall love the Lord your God with your whole heart, with your whole soul, and with all your mind. This is the greatest and the first commandment. The second is like it: You shall love your neighbor as yourself. On these two commandments the whole Law is based, and the Prophets as well" (Mt 22:37-40).

Once, while I was walking toward the historic Jewish synagogue in Toledo, in Spain, two Israeli girls walked past me. As we approached the synagogue, one of them said: "Wouldn't it be wonderful to hear some Hebrew spoken here!" The temptation was too great to be resisted, and to their great surprise and delight I obligingly cried out "Shalom!" The word means "peace" or "greetings" and was often on Jesus' lips.

To know that the names of the archangels mentioned in the Bible can be translated is another little satisfaction anyone can experience. "Michael" means "Who is like God?" "Gabriel" (Gibbor+el) means "Strong One of God;" and "Raphael" (Raph+el) means, "God heals."

St. Jerome (d. 420), educated in the rhetorical schools of Rome and a great lover of the classics, was the first westerner to learn Hebrew. He did so under the tutelage of a rabbi who, like Nicodemus (as he said), came to him by night for fear of his fellow Jews. In a famous letter, Jerome explains how much it cost him to learn Hebrew:

> After having studied the pointed style of Quintilian, the fluency of Cicero, the weightiness of Fronto, the gentleness of Pliny, I now began to learn the alphabet again, and practice harsh and guttural words. What efforts I spent on that task, what difficulties I had to face, how often I despaired, how often I gave up, and then in my eagerness to learn began again, my own knowledge can witness from personal experience, and those can testify who were then living with me! I thank the Lord that from a bitter seed of learning, I am now plucking sweet fruits.

The sweet fruits of which Jerome spoke were his translations of the Old Testament books, the Vulgate. Through this achievement the West came to know the Old Testament, and the Vulgate served the Church well for more than a thousand years.

The Targums

The sacred books, written and read in the synagogues in the Hebrew tongue, became increasingly difficult to comprehend by congregations which spoke only Aramaic. There thus came into being the edifying paraphrases and translations which are called *targums*. The most famous of the Palestinian targums is that of Onkelos, which contained the Pentateuch. The T. Jonathan treated the prophets. Both works go back to the second century (fragments of targums have been found at Qumran) but in their present form they date to the fourth or fifth century A. D.

By reason of their antiquity, they have some value for the text of the Bible; as paraphrases, however, they are to be handled with reservations. They are mentioned merely to show how the Old Testament has been studied across the centuries.

The Talmudic Writings

Talmud is a word which means "study" or "teaching." It is the name given to that body of writings which contains the pharisaic oral traditions and regulations that we read about in the gospels. The two main divisions of the Talmud are the *Mishnah* (subdivided into the Mishnah proper and the *Tosephta,* or "supplement") and the *Gemarah,* the Aramaic "completion" of the Mishnah. The Mishnah (or "repetition") and Tosephta are divided into six and four *seder* or *parts* respectively. These in turn are divided into treatises or tracts, and then into chapters. In all there are 63 tracts and 525 chapters.

The Talmud was not committed to writing until the third century A.D. From this fact alone, the Bible reader must proceed with caution, lest he be tempted to apply the codified laws of the Talmud back to New Testament times. It would be extremely injudicious, to say the least, to declare, as did some older Lives of Christ, that the trial of Jesus was carried out in violation of existing Jewish law. Those laws may not even have been in force two hundred years before their codification. Furthermore, the Talmud is primarily a collection of opinions and not a digested corpus of law as we understand it.

In these writings, two distinct tones prevail: one, derived from the Hebrew word "to go," is *halakic,* or legalistic; the second is *haggadic* in tone (the term means "narration"), and contains stories, moral reflections, maxims, and observations on many subjects. The chief purpose of the *Haggadah* was to edify and inspire the reader, and to awaken in him those finer qualities of heart and mind that are called for by the *Halakah.**

---

*The reader may wish to pursue this further, and may consult H. L. Strack, *Introduction to the Talmud and Midrash* (Atheneum pb, 1969).

RABBIS AND RABBINICAL LITERATURE

The Rabbis ("heads" or "masters"):

The *Sopherim:* These were the scribes or the "bookmen" who succeeded Ezra. They wrote and counted out the words of the Torah. They were in turn succeeded by great teachers like Shammai and Hillel (first century B.C.).

The *Tannaim* were the "repeaters" or teachers of the oral traditions.

The *Amoraim* were the "expositors" or "explainers" of the tradition. They appeared from the third to the fifth century A.D.

The *Saboraim*, or "thinkers" fit into the sixth and seventh centuries.

The *Masoretes* were "traditionalists." The Masoretic Period extended from roughly 500-1000 (or even 1300) A.D.

The *Karaites* were those who followed the Scriptures, as opposed to those who followed the oral law of the Talmud. From 767 A.D. on.

The *Geonim*, or heads of academies ("eminences"), flourished between the ninth and eleventh centuries. They were named after the famous Saadia ben Joseph (892-942).

Maimonides, Moses (1135-1204) enjoyed a special esteem, expressed in the saying: "From Moses to Moses, there is no one like Moses." His well-known mnemonic is *Rambam*, which stands for *R*abbi *M*oses *b*en *M*oses.

Kimhi, David (1160-1235) or *Radak* (for Rabbi David Kimhi).

The Rabbinical Literature

The *Talmud:* "study" or "learning." The Talmudic Period proper is fixed by some from the mid-third to the sixth centuries. The two major divisions of the Talmud are:

The *Mishnah:* "repetition" of the oral teachings of the ages. The Tosephta are "supplements or additions" to the Mishnah.

The *Gemarah:* "completion" or commentaries on the Mishnah.

Styles in the Literature

1) The *Halakhah*, the legal material (second-sixth centuries) of the Talmud.

2) The *Haggadah* (third-sixth centuries), moralistic stories instilling loyalty to Jewish traditions and ideals.

The Masoretes

In the sixth century A.D. there appeared a guild of trained scholars known as the Masoretes. *Masorah* means "tradition" and, as their name indicates, the Masoretes' chief concern was to preserve the sacred text. The text itself was sacrosanct, and they considered it their task to hand it down to the next generation completely unchanged. They counted the words of the Torah and noted the total at the end of each book; they also gave the middle word of each book to facilitate checking. If a copy of the Law failed to match these numbers, it was rejected—there was to be no carelessness in the handing down of the sacred writings. As a result, there came into being what is known as the Masoretic Text, which was as close to being a standard text as was then possible. The common abbreviation for it is MT.

This reverence for the text was carried to unusual lengths, for even the obvious mistakes—a letter off line, a letter written backwards—were carefully preserved. Textual errors were allowed to stand unchanged, but a tiny circle over the mistaken letter would indicate that the mistake had been noted, and that one could find the proper spelling or word in the margin. Thus two words *kethiv* and *qere* acquire a special meaning: *kethiv* means what is *written* in the text (the mistake), and *qere* means what the text *ought* to read. There are some 1300 marginal corrections of this sort in the Masoretic Text. (One will recall that a similar word, *Koran,* the sacred writing of the Moslems, means "read.") Also found in the margin are notes on the occurrence of words, features of the writing, directions for pronunciation, variant readings, and other textual information.

For all their resolve to hand down the sacred writings intact, the Masoretes sometimes wavered, and their reverence for the text yielded to theological scruples. The text of Gn 18:22, for example, was changed, because it was deemed improper that the Lord should stand *before Abraham.* Harsh and shocking statements were softened by euphemisms; the advice given to

Job by his wife: "Curse God and die," became "Bless God and die" (2:9). At other times the changes reflect the contempt the Hebrews felt for idolatry; thus the name Meribaal and Ishbaal were changed to Meribosheth and Ishbosheth, making the despised Baal *a thing of shame*—the meaning of *bosheth*.

The best of the Masoretic Texts is the one attributed to Rabbi ben Asher (930 A.D.) The great Maimonides approved it, and it was used as the basis of modern critical editions of the Masoretic Text.* Up to the discovery of the Dead Sea Scrolls in 1947, which provides a text that dates from the first century of our era, the oldest Masoretic Text had been the tenth century Codex Babylonicus Petropolitanus. The earliest printed Hebrew Bible dates to 1477 for the Psalms, and 1488 for the remaining books. (There was some resistance at first to subjecting the holy writings to the mindless printing press.)

The Midrashim

Midrash means "to seek" (see 2 Chr 13:22). The Midrashim are not part of the Talmud but rather running commentaries on the Old Testament. They were usually narrative or haggadic in tone, that is, they aimed at instructing and edifying the reader. Examples of a reflective adaptation of ancient texts appear in Prv 1-9; Is 55-66; Sir 44-60, Wis 16-19.

As a result of renewed interest in the Infancy Narratives of the first two gospels, a lively debate on the nature of these chapters has developed. Some consider them as pious and inventive embellishments and not truly historical, that is, they are Christian midrash. There has been no great rush to approve this view, but a midrash is not necessarily fiction, or para-historical. It can be a reflection on ancient Scriptures in the light of actual fact, or a kind of "reading the Bible by the Bible" while dealing with more recent fact. Perhaps the essence of the midrash is that it adapts something ancient to the present.

---

*The standard Masoretic Text today is Kittel's *Biblia Hebraica* (ed. P. Kahle, Stuttgart, 1951).

Many good biblical scholars insist that the gospels do not fit easily into the category of midrash, the purpose of which was to make the Old Testament intelligible and applicable to the reader. This is not the aim of the infancy narratives. These were written, as Raymond Brown says, "to make Jesus' origins intelligible against the background of the fulfillment of Old Testament expectations." (See his *The Birth of the Messiah*, p. 36f, and the Appendix, p. 557-563, where he writes on "Midrash as a Literary Genre.")

The Samaritan Pentateuch

The ancient practice of transplanting conquered peoples (see 2 Kgs 17:24-41) resulted in a great mixing of bloods. After the return from Exile, devout Jews, who looked upon intermarriage with horror, took drastic measures to purge the Chosen People of alien blood. Jews who had not been carried off into exile had married non-Jewish women from Ashdod, Ammon, Moab, and elsewhere. They were expelled from the Jerusalem community (Ezr 9-10; Neh 13:23-30) unless they gave up these wives and children. One of those who refused to do this was Manasseh, grandson of the highpriest Eliashib. He lost no time in setting up a rival temple on Mt. Garizim, which is near modern Naplus. The temple had an altar of holocausts, and priests to serve it. They also had a copy of the Law of Moses which Manasseh had carried with him from Jerusalem.

This schism or break occurred around 432 B.C., causing an animosity which time did not heal. The Samaritan woman at the well (Jn 4) expressed astonishment that Jesus even spoke to her, and the apostles were harshly treated because they were obviously travelling toward Jerusalem on pilgrimage (Lk 9:51-53).

A small enclave of Samaritans, numbering a few hundred, exists still at Naplus. Those who visit Jacob's Well there are shown a scroll and informed that it was written by Abisha, Moses' great-grandson. This scroll is the Samaritan Pentateuch, written in archaic letters, but quite clearly—to judge from the script—a mere 700 years old. The text contains a number of textual alterations which serve to justify the existence of the Samaritan community. Even so, it represents a Hebrew text preserved and developed outside the mainstream of Jewish orthodoxy. Good critical editions of the Masoretic Text note these variations in the footnotes.

Aramaic

After the Exile, a new language spread throughout the Near East. It was Aramaic, a North Semitic tongue, similar to Hebrew in form but different. It became the international commercial language sometime after 500 B.C., and by the first century B.C. it was the ordinary language spoken by the people living in the Fertile Crescent. There is an interesting story about an exchange between Rabsaces, Sennacherib's envoy, and the representative of Hezekiah at the time when the Assyrian seemed about to capture the latter's city (2 Kgs 18:17ff). Speaking in Hebrew, Rabsaces pointed out the futility of resistance, and called for surrender. The authorities on the walls of the city urged the commander: "Please speak to your servants in Aramaic; we understand it. Do not speak to us in Judean, within earshot of the people who are on the wall!" Naturally their naive request was ignored. The interest of the story lies in the fact that it helps establish a date after which Aramaic was commonly spoken. Sennacherib's invasion dates to ca 700 B.C.

Aramaic stands to Hebrew more or less as modern English does to Elizabethan English. The letters are the same, many words are identical, but the changes are so many and so profound that the two are different. The following passages of the Old Testament are in Aramaic: Gn 31:47; Jer 10:11; Dn 2:4b-7:28; Ezr 4:7-6:18; 7:12-26. The largest single corpus of Aramaic writing outside the Bible was discovered in 1903 at Elephantine, in Egypt (see p. 175-6), and dates to the fifth century B.C.

Syriac is the most notable of the various dialects which developed from the Aramaic.

Biblical Greek

The peoples of ancient Hellas spoke many dialects, one of which, the Attic, eventually prevailed over the Ionic, Doric, and Aeolian dialects to become what is known as classical Greek. From the fifth century B.C. on for almost a thousand years, Greek was the international language both of the Middle East and of the West. Two of the Old Testament books, Wisdom and 2 Maccabees, were written in Greek, as were all of the New Testament books with the possible exception of a primitive Matthew, which may have been composed in Aramaic.

New Testament Greek differs so greatly from the classical tongue of Demosthenes and Euripides that for a long time it was considered to be a corrupt form of that language. Not only does it have a strong Semitic flavor, but also many bizarre forms. Certain outstanding characteristics of classical Greek, such as long elegant periods and those particles by which complicated sentences could be accurately and harmoniously balanced, were conspicuous by their absence in New Testament Greek. The optative tense was missing, and interspersed with the Greek were many "loan-words."

It was not until the discovery of vast quantities of papyri toward the end of the nineteenth century that a better understanding was gained of New Testament Greek. Adolf Deissmann (1866-1937) was the first to perceive that New Testament Greek, with its Semitic background, was the language of the man in the street, of soldiers in their barracks, of tradesmen in the marketplace. This accounted for its freshness, warmth, terseness, and color, and also for the puzzling differences in morphology, syntax, and vocabulary. To indicate that this was a special kind of language, it was given the name of *Koine*, or "common" Greek. It was the spoken language of that day.

With today's revival of interest in ancient languages, one may at least hope that some readers will take advantage of the critical editions of the Greek New Testament now available. (See p.

146). Many beauties and subtleties of the Greek almost defy translation. For example, the nuance between the imperfect (denoting an action going on in the past) and the aorist (signifying an action completed in the past) cannot be indicated in English. The use of the subjunctive mood, the cases of nouns, and the subtle implications of these are practically lost in English.

It is curious that the Greek language survived in the West until the long controversies over the Incarnation and Trinity were thoroughly debated and given accurate expression.

There are now such abundant aids to the study of biblical languages that the biblical scholar, who by neglecting them deprives himself of access to the original texts, cannot avoid the charge of superficiality and neglect.

NINE

THE CONTRIBUTION OF ARCHAEOLOGY

Few things can so kindle the admiration of modern man as the gigantic pyramids, royal palaces, and beautiful artifacts of ancient times. Assurbanipal, ruler of Assyria 2500 years ago, marvelled as he pored over enigmatic inscriptions on clay tablets ages older than he. Nabonidus (sixth century B.C.) had soundings made at the base of the age-old ziggurat that dominated the Mesopotamian plain. This interest and curiosity have continued. Schliemann's rediscovery of ancient Troy (1871) and Carter's finding of the tomb of King Tutankhamon (1922) excited the whole world. But nothing engenders such excitement as discoveries that touch on the Bible—periodic "sightings" of Noah's Ark on a mountain top, or Garstang's layer of "clay deposited by the Flood," for example, receive wide publicity. And for good reason. The Bible is not only an old and interesting book; it deals with and speaks to Everyman.

Biblical archaeology is a relatively new science. It started in earnest after World War I, when the British General Allenby drove the Turks from the Holy Land.* Exploration of the biblical lands was pioneered by the intrepid Edward Robinson in

*Allenby's name sounds like the Arabic *al-nebi*, or "the prophet." The general was urged to enter the city of Jerusalem through the Gate Beautiful, as a conqueror. Instead, like a pilgrim, he removed his shoes and entered the Holy City barefooted.

1838 and 1852. The year 1865 saw the establishment of the Palestine Exploration Fund, and under P. Lagrange the Ecole Biblique et Archéologique Française opened its doors in 1890. After the Armistice (1918), the American School of Oriental Research became an important archaeological center under the long leadership of William F. Albright (1919-39). The names of these men and their schools began to appear wherever solid, scientific research was being done.

The field of biblical archaeology is immense, taking in all the lands of the Fertile Crescent. Thus included are Mesopotamia, Syria, Palestine, Egypt, and the adjoining countries of Moab, Edom, and Ammon. One never knows where archaeological lightning will strike next, and all these places have yielded bits and scraps of information which contribute to a better understanding of life in ancient times. Such information is valuable, as it makes the Bible more intelligible.

One interesting by-product of this type of research is that it shows the Bible up in a good light—the genuine Egyptian flavor of some parts of Genesis, notably the Joseph story,* is now recognized, and the Hebrew wisdom books are known to contain echoes of the wisdom of other sages.** As for the myths and epics of Sumeria and Akkad, it is obvious that the Hebrew outlook on life and death, on man's origins, and on sin resemble them in part but are decidedly superior to them in content and quality.

In order to read the Bible as it ought to be read, one should spend some time on the archaeology of the Near East. It will be a mind-expanding experience, introducing the reader to some of the greatest political and religious cultures the world has known.

Palestine or Israel is the land of the Bible par excellence. The

---

*The Hyksos, a warlike people who used horse-drawn chariots, ruled over Egypt from ca 1700-1580 B.C. Joseph's exalted rank was more likely under a foreign dynasty, such as the Hyksos, who brought Syria and Palestine into the theatre of international history.

**See for example Prv 22:17-23:11, which are clearly based on the Egyptian maxims of Amen-emophis.

contours of the land, the seas and rivers and sites of cities, have changed little since Bible times. Camel caravans are still to be seen there, and ancient customs—where oil and TV and technology have not driven them out—still persist. A line from Faulkner, used to describe the South, aptly applies to the Holy Land: "The past is not dead there, it isn't even past!"

After a visit to the Holy Land—an unforgettable experience—one reads the Bible with new eyes. New discoveries of course will be made; that is the business of archaeology. To help the reader cope with the literature of archaeology, we now briefly explain some of the terms currently used in archaeological circles.

1. A *tell* is a mound or hillock that was once inhabited by man. It is readily identified by a peculiar feature: its top is visibly flat. As earthquake, invasion, or the inroads of time visited the site, city walls fell and new ones rose from their rubble. This happened many times. The tells generally boasted access to water, proximity to arable land, and a location that could be easily fortified and defended. Some of the better sites such as Jericho (known as T. es-Sultan, or "The Big Tell") have been inhabited almost uninterruptedly since very ancient times.

2. The Arabic word *khirbet* means a *ruin*. The best-known ruins today are perhaps those of Kh. Qumran, of which we shall speak later.

3. *Wadi*, another Arabic word, refers to a dry gulch or river bed. During the rainy season, wadis become sudden torrents and are capable of great destruction. One reason for this is that the soil of the Holy Land is of a poor quality called marl; when rain falls on it, a sort of film only millimeters deep develops, and the water runs off without sinking into the ground. The speed of a winter "torrent" is awe-inspiring; there are known incidents of it overtaking a horse at full gallop. Among the many wadis, one of the best known is W. Kidron which runs past the Garden of Gethsemani, and W. Murabba'at below Qumran.

4. *Jebel,* the Arabic word for mountain, is abbreviated by J. or

sometimes Dj. (for Djebel). J. Mousa is the mountain of Moses, or Sinai.

5. The Bible contains many reference to Canaanite *highplaces*, called *bama* or *bamoth* in Hebrew (1 Sm 9:12-20). The highplaces were pagan in origin. A god coming down to earth would logically first come into contact with a highplace. Unusual features of certain sites, a peculiar rock formation, a spring, or perhaps a tree growing where no tree should—were interpreted as signs of a divine visitation. Here then would be a good spot to contact a god. A prominent feature of the highplaces were upright sculptured stone slabs or pillars, called *steles* or *stelas*. Phallic in origin, they represented the god Baal, whose consort, the female *Asherah*, was represented by upright wooden stakes variously called *posts, stocks,* or *sacred groves*. These symbols of the fertility goddess were set up opposite the steles. This was the crude, sensuous culture which greeted the Israelites as they entered the land of promise. The Israelites were attracted by it, of course, but strongly opposed to it in principle—Yahweh, their God, had no consort. The author of 2 Kings would later praise Hezekiah because he sought to destroy the highplaces and do away with the sacred prostitution that flourished there. There were, to be sure, some "bad" kings during whose reigns the highplaces flourished.

6. *Shephelah* or *negev* are terms increasingly familiar to us as the state of Israel pursues its policy of using Hebrew as its official language. Shephelah refers to the fertile western plain of the land, while Negev describes the land to the south of Hebron.

7. *Shards and potsherds*. Ancient kings were usually buried in royal spendor, and grave robbers plied a profitable underground business. Few buried monarchs retained their treasures for long. In Palestine, however, little of marketable value has shown up, with the exception of some ivory bedstead carvings at Megiddo. No hoards of gold or silver or precious jewels gladden the excavators; instead, they everywhere run into broken pieces of clay pots, or shards.

It was an Englishman, Sir Flinders Petrie, who first saw that archaeologists were overlooking another kind of treasure—the omnipresent shard. Each shard, Petrie reasoned, was a mute witness to the past, and had something to say about the slice of time it represented. Thus was born the method of sequence-dating, which Petrie introduced at T. el-Hesi in 1894. He began to reconstruct the original pots from fragments. In time, a backlog of sizes and shapes enabled the scholars to trace the evolution of pottery. First there were crude but useful vases, but with time craftsmen achieved a considerable degree of sophistication, and the pots combined both function and beauty. (Of this, Nabatean pottery is an outstanding example.) The texture of the clay, the shape of the vessel, and the addition of glazes and stylish decor enable the practiced eye to assign an age for the shard, confidently labelling it as a product of the Bronze, Iron, or other age.

Pottery thus enables us to know something about the culture and history of a vanished people. For example, the lower a stratum, the more ancient it is, and each level contains its quota of shards. The archaeologist may note that shards on an upper stratum are clearly inferior to those on a lower level. This may indicate that the city had been taken by uncultured marauders who settled upon the ruins of the conquered city. That they knew little of the arts such as pottery is quite evident from the kind of debris they left behind.

From a practical point of view, this is of some importance. The date of the Exodus is a very old problem. Two dates claim attention: 1550 B.C., and 1250 B.C. The first date can be maintained, but not without difficulty; the second has much to recommend it, for at Jericho (the Israelite point-of-entry) there is a clear cultural break between the levels of the Bronze Age (which ends ca 1200 B.C.) and the Iron Age (which begins then). Perhaps this cultural break can be explained by the arrival of a nomadic desert people quite unacquainted with the arts that grace a city.

From what has been said, the value of the lowly shard should be clear. The shard is to archaeologists what fossils are to geologists. It seems superfluous to say that the shard has to be interpreted with prudence, and many other considerations must be taken into account before drawing far-reaching conclusions. A leeway of from fifty to a hundred years must be allowed for in any case, inasmuch as cultural changes (especially in styles of household ware) are ordinarily slow.

8. A shard with writing on it is called an *ostracon* (pl. *ostraca*). Our word *ostracize* comes from the ancient practice of using clay fragments as ballots. (A "Yes" could mean another term in office for the incumbent; a "No" meant banishment or exile.) Up until 1965, fifteen Aramaic ostraca were known to exist, but in that year ninety more were found at T. Arad. The so-called Lachish Letters (see p. 179) were ostraca which spoke of the beginning of the Chaldean siege of that city; they date to the sixth century B.C.

Excavations of Biblical Interest

One day I was showing a British officer some of the books in the library at the Ecole Biblique in Jerusalem. When he saw pictures of the papyri and learned how the scholars had painstakingly reassembled the fragments and pieced out the texts, he began to shake his head. "One half of the world," he muttered, "doesn't know what the other half is doing."

The next few pages will attempt to inform the reader about archaeological undertakings which in one way or another bear upon the Bible. Whole books have been written about each of these excavations. But first, a few preliminary remarks.

Modern archaeologists are no longer treasure hunters, as were many of the earlier diggers. Great museums in London, Paris, and Germany proudly display ancient artifacts taken by the shipload from Greece, Persia, Egypt, and other lands. That has all drastically changed. Each country now has a vigilant Department of Antiquities which controls all permits to dig, and carefully sees to it that most of the finds will remain in that particular country. Even in the United States, the Antiquities Act of 1906 protects historic and prehistoric ruins and monuments on federal lands. One can readily sympathize with such precautions.

A modern archaeological campaign is a business-like affair, a costly undertaking requiring permits; transportation; special equipment such as surveying instruments, cameras, special tools; and a small army of select personnel: scholars, historians, linguists, photographers, and artists. Archaeologists have a great passion for detail and a great need for sound judgment. They always seek that discovery of something that contributes to a clearer picture of the past. Biblical archaeology does not prove or disprove, but in fact often supports the Bible by casting light upon its background. (To locate these sites, see map p. 10.)

The Rosetta Stone (1799)

During Napoleon's sojourn in Egypt, a black basalt stone was discovered at Rosetta (modern Rashid) on the western delta of the Nile. The original stone now rests in the British Museum, but many replicas are found elsewhere. The stone is important because of its trilingual inscription, the first in hieroglyphic, the second in demotic (a streamlined cursive form of hieroglyphic), and the third in Greek.

Champollion, a Frenchman (1790-1832) and his son were able to use the stone to decipher hieroglyphics, the ancient Egyptian writing. They knew what the stone said from the Greek part of the inscription; this they were able to use to translate the hieroglyphics. The three inscriptions were all the same, that is, they commemorated the accession of Ptolemy V Epiphanes (203-181 B.C.) to the throne.

Biblical interest? As the Rosetta Stone enabled scholars to read other and older Egyptian inscriptions, a curious fact emerged. Nowhere in any of these inscriptions was there mention made of the Exodus, the mass departure of foreign slaves. One would think that the loss of 600,000 people might have been recorded. Two possible explanations come to mind. The

Egyptians did not record disastrous defeats, but only victories. Or perhaps the Israelites were not really that numerous as they left the land of Egypt.

The Behistun Inscription (1835)

Behistun is modern Bisutun, in Iran. During the first part of the nineteenth century, a young English diplomat, Major Henry Creswicke Rawlinson (1810-1895) espied, on the side of a cliff 225 feet above the plain, an intriguing group of figures and what appeared to be columns of writing. In the best tradition of the English colonial servant, Rawlinson had developed an interest in the country to which he had been assigned, had studied its history and learned its language. So he climbed the cliff, and copied out the inscription. It turned out to be something of a Rosetta Stone, having on it inscriptions in three different languages. These proved to be Akkadian, Elamite, and Old Persian. Translating the Persian was easy, and provided a clue to the other inscriptions: all three told of a victory gained by Darius I Hystaspes (522-486 B.C.) over the rebel Gautama and his allies.

Rawlinson's translation of the hitherto unreadable cuneiform writing opened the door to a vast literature. In this particular inscription no mention is made of Israel, but the knowledge of cuneiform which it made possible has been of tremendous value in reconstructing the background—especially religious background—of much of the Old Testament. Knowing how to read cuneiform has made modern man a contemporary of Hammurabi, and of the people of Mari, Nuzu, Ugarit, and even Egypt.

Fortunately we have at our disposal a fine collection of all these texts in J. B. Pritchard's anthologies of texts and pictures (see bibliography).

The Moabite Stone (1868)

Also called the Stele of Mesha, this stone was discovered at Dibon in what is now Jordan. Its discoverer was a Lutheran minister named Klein. Unable to move the stone, he proceeded, with the help of the Frenchman Clermont-Ganneau, to make a "squeeze" of the inscription on the stone. They smeared wet paper over the inscription, and peeled it off after it had dried. This gave them a negative of the inscription. (Modern archaeologists use plastic sprays for the same purpose.) It was fortunate that they had acted as they did, for when they had gone away, the inhabitants of the area, fearful that the foreigners had put a magic spell on the stone, built a fire around it and then dashed cold water over it, causing it to break into many pieces. Thanks to the squeeze, however, both the stone and its inscription could be reconstructed.

The Moabite Stone is important in that it is extrabiblical evidence of the importance of King Omri of Israel (885-874 B.C.),whom Mesha had defeated in battle. Until the appearance of the Lachish Letters (1932), the Stone was the only extrabiblical source to mention the name of Yahweh.

The Siloam Inscription (1880)

With tantalizing brevity (see 2 Kgs 20:20 and 2 Chr 32:2-4, 30) the Bible relates Hezekiah's concern about a water supply in case of a siege, and how he managed to insure that Jerusalem would have that water. For centuries the spring of Gihon on the eastern flank of Ophel (David's original city) was Jerusalem's only source of water, apart from what was gathered into cisterns during the rainy season. What Hezekiah did was to dig a tunnel through the rock, bringing the water from Gihon to the pool of Siloam inside the walls. (This pool is still used today.) An inscription describing his engineering feat was accidentally discovered when a flashlight was aimed from inside the tunnel back toward the opening into the pool. The light revealed six lines (apparently the latter half of the original inscription) which told how the work had begun at both ends and how the workmen had met in the middle. The tunnel took the shape of a big "S" and was about 1750 feet in length. A good drop of 7'2'' assured a steady flow. The project was completed in less than

200 days, a remarkable accomplishment.

Hezekiah's Tunnel sparked the Parker Expedition to the Holy Land—one of the most unusual of all expeditions. The story is amusing, and so indicative of both human enthusiasm and smallness that it deserves retelling. The central figure in it was an English intelligence officer, Montagu B. Parker. Accompanied by a Finn named Juvelius, Parker arrived in Jerusalem in 1910 along with a small army of 179 Welsh miners with carbide lamps on their hats. The miners were directed by Juvelius, who claimed to have found and deciphered a biblical cryptogram describing the location of the treasures of David and Solomon. Thus motivated, the miners ventured into the mysterious opening into which the waters of Gihon flowed.

What the Parker Expedition did, actually, was to give Hezekiah's tunnel its first thorough cleaning in centuries. No treasure was found, of course, but Parker was not a man to be easily discouraged. With the connivance of a night watchman, he began secret digs under the Dome of the Rock, the Islamic mosque in Jerusalem. But secrets are hard to keep in Jerusalem. Parker's American rival—a man who had planned to explore the tunnel with the help of a Rockefeller grant—arrived on the scene only to find Parker already there. So he hired strong-lunged Arabs to run throught the streets at night, crying out "Why do you sleep? The infidel is desecrating your sanctuary!" In the ensuing uproar, the members of the Parker Expedition had to flee for their lives. That was the end of the *affaire Parker*.

The brighter side to this bizarre adventure was the publication of P. Vincent's *Jérusalem sous terre*. He also kept readers of the *Revue biblique* informed about the day-by-day work in the tunnel.

Even before Parker, Gihon and its reservoir had attracted the attention of Sir Charles Warren and Sgt. Birtles of the British Royal Engineers. They noted and climbed partway up a shaft (technically called a *sinnor*, and found also at Gibeon and Megiddo) over the back part of the retaining pool (See Is 22:11;

Sir 48:17). Almost fifty years later, Parker and his men cleared the shaft, and one of his workmen easily climbed up to the top. This seems to clear up one of those tersely stated biblical puzzles, namely, how Joab managed to deliver the city of the Jebusites into David's hands. He simply went up the unguarded shaft (which assured the beleaguered Jebusites water), and threw open the gates of the city for David's waiting warriors (see 2 Sm 5:6f; 1 Chr 11:6; 2 Chr 32:4).

The diagram below will help the reader visualize what took place.

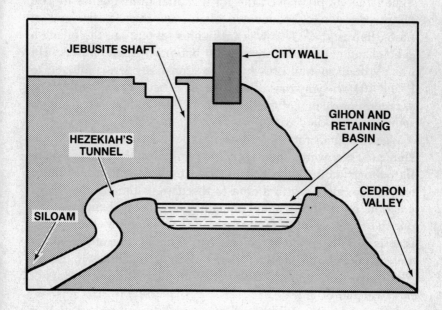

The Tell El-Amarna Tablets (1887)

These tablets were found at T. el-Amarna, a site some 300 miles north of ancient Karnak and Luxor. Most of them are anguished letters from the mid-fourteenth century B.C. written in cuneiform by Canaanite scribes to Pharaoh Amenhotep III and his son Akhenaton. The burden of the letters, which come mostly from Palestine and Syria, was that "my lord, the king" had better bestir himself and take action against ever more audacious enemies, or he would lose his cities. People were not paying their tribute, and the Apiru (also spelled Habiru) seemed bent on taking over the land. The letters of Abdu-heba, governor of Jerusalem, were especially urgent.

The Amarna Letters went largely unanswered. The Pharaoh Akhenaton, the husband of Nefertiti of legendary beauty, was a religious reformer with other concerns on his mind. In order to escape the smothering power of the god Amon and his priests, Akhenaton simply moved the royal capital from Thebes to Tell el-Amarna, where he devoted all his energies to the cult of Aton, the sun disc. This was a religious revolution; the pharaoh even changed his name from *Amen*-hotep IV to Akhen-*Aton*. He was a gifted poet and his hymn to Aton has been compared to Psalm 104; the Amarna religion has also been called with some exaggeration a monotheistic religion. But Akhenaton's reform seems to have died with him.

What intrigues the Bible reader is the mention of the Apiru or Habiru. They were, apparently, "a people on the move." Were they the Israelites who had just fled from Egypt? Could these letters provide us with a clue to the date of the Exodus? This position, once briefly maintained, has now been abandoned. To put the Exodus in the fourteenth or even fifteenth century B.C. is to ignore the voice of archaeology, which says nothing about any major cultural change taking place at that time in Israel. The Apiru were more probably marauders, or simply drifters of no particular origin.

The hopes of the Bible reader for extrabiblical confirmation of the Exodus here have been dashed. But at the same time, this glimpse into the religious and political life of Egypt has been rewarding in itself.

The Stela of Merneptah (1897)

Discovered at Thebes by Sir Flinders Petrie, the "Israel Stela" records the boast of Merneptah (1224-1214 B.C.), written in hieroglyphic, that he had "humbled Israel." This the only reference made to Israel in all Egyptian epigraphy and, oddly enough, there is missing the customary determinative sign of "land." The text then can stand for an unsettled, or nomadic people. The time is right for the Exodus, but the argument drawn from the missing sign should not be pushed too far.

The Code of Hammurabi (1901)

The name of Hammurabi, who reigned for forty-two years as king of Babylon (1728-1686 B.C.), is attached to a famous code of laws inscribed upon a block of black stone that is 7′6″ in height. It was found at Susa, where it had been carried as a trophy of war; De Morgan, its discoverer, brought it to the Louvre as a trophy of archaeology. Written in cuneiform, the code contains 282 items covering a wide variety of cases, and similar in many respects to laws which later appeared in the Pentateuch. The Code is now recognized as having been a reform, not an original creation, of Babylonian laws. The text was quickly published in translation by P. Scheil, O.P., in 1902.

Following the discovery of the Code of Hammurabi, a wave of excitement stirred the world of biblical scholarship. Was Hammurabi perhaps to be identified with the Amraphel of Genesis 14:1, so that Abraham was his contemporary who robbed the king of his booty? But the similarity of names is quite weak, calling for unexplainable changes in the orthography of the name Hammurabi. And historically, the identification would leave something to be desired—to put Hammurabi that far back in the nineteeth century B.C. creates a gap of more than a century in Babylonian history. The excitement was soon over. But the find did help. The Bible story and many of its laws are now known to fit well into conditions prevailing in the nineteeth century B.C.

The Elephantine Papyri (1903)

Aswan, famous now for its dam, was once an important frontier post and a flourishing center of the ivory trade. Opposite

Aswan is an island in the Nile known as Elephantine (in Greek), or Yeb (in Aramaic). Here, quite by accident, some sixty Aramaic papyri were discovered in 1903. They revealed the presence there of Jewish colonists and their families, serving probably as mercenaries under a Persian governor in the fifth century B.C. The papyri inform us of letters written from the island to Johanan, the high priest of Jerusalem, requesting clarification: could they rebuild a temple at Elephantine to replace the one recently destroyed by the Egyptians? The Jerusalem authorities apparently ignored the request, since a temple built anywhere but in Jerusalem would have violated the prescription of Dt 12:6. After an interval, then, the Elephantines addressed other letters to Sanballat, the governor of Samaria, asking for permission and assistance. This time there was a reply—the temple might be rebuilt, but only meal-offerings and incense could be tolerated at the altar. (The names Johanan and Sanballat appear in Neh 12:22; 2:19.)

Serabit El-Khadim (1904)

At this site, some fifty miles west of the traditional site of Mt. Sinai, Sir Flinders Petrie discovered, on the walls of an ancient turquoise mine, proto-Sinaitic inscriptions which date back to 1840-1790 B.C. Seemingly based on Egyptian hieroglyphics, the writing is paleo-Semitic, and points to the emergence of an alphabet from which first the Hebrew and Phoenician, and ultimately the Greek, Latin, and English alphabets developed.

Boghazkoy (1907)

The existence of an immense Hittite empire which lasted from 1800-1200 B.C. was revealed by the discovery and subsequent decipherment (1915) of the cuneiform tablets found at Hattush in 1907. Cuneiform was used for many languages; this one ran from left to right (an Indo-European feature) and used vowels. What makes these texts so important is the fact that they describe various kinds of treaties (i.e., parity and suzerainty treaties) which help our understanding of the Hebrew notion of covenant. (See pp. 8-11.)

The Hittites or Hethites, also called the Hatti, appear frequently in the Bible. Abraham dealt with them when he purchased land with trees on it, near Hebron, to bury Sarah (see Gn 23). The story of Uriah the Hittite is well known (2 Sm 11); Solomon had Hittite wives (1 Kgs 11) and had dealings with Hittite kings (1 Kgs 10:29). But the extent of the Hittite empires was not suspected until the discovery of these texts.

The Gezer Calendar (1908)

This small limestone tablet was discovered by Macalister at Gezer. It throws light on Palestinian agricultural practices as far back as the tenth century B.C.. It is one of the earliest important Hebrew inscriptions.

Ahiram of Byblos (1923)

The town of Byblos (modern Jebeil), twenty miles north of modern Beirut, was once used as a jumping-off place for warlike expeditions against Mesopotamia. Thutmoses III and other Egyptian kings were acquainted with Byblos and its excellent harbor. It is more famous, however, for the stone coffin of Ahiram which was found there; the inscription which runs around its cover is important because it is the first recognizable alphabetic writing known. A date around 1000 B.C. is assigned to it.

The reader will note that Byblos appears in the Bible as Gebal, and that our word for book or Bible derives from Byblos. The city, a prize coveted by many kings, was mentioned often in ancient literatures. One would hardly suspect its importance from the scant attention given it in the Bible (Jos 13:5; 1 Kgs 5:32; Ezk 27:9).

The Nuzu Tablets (1925)

East of the Tigris, not far from modern Kirkuk, lie the ruins of ancient Nuzu or Nuzi. The center of a non-Semitic people called the Hurri (in the Bible, Horites), Nuzu once exercised a great influence upon its neighbors. The 3000 tablets discovered here contained business contracts, court records, and details about family life. Many biblical practices parallel those in these tablets. Thus, the tablets too speak of the practice of adopting a slave as a son under certain circumstances (see Gn 15:2-4); of a sterile wife giving her maid-servant to her husband (see Gn 16:1-2), and of the painful dilemma the arrival of a son to the first wife could cause (see Gn 21). At Nuzu, as in the story of Jacob and Rachel (Gn 31), the possession of the family idols or *teraphim* constituted a solid claim to inheritance.

The Nuzu Tablets therefore throw light upon many Israelite practices, showing that the Bible rings true, and that it is no longer the only witness to customs in vogue during the second millenium B.C.

Ras Shamra—Ancient Ugarit (1928)

Ras Shamra is situated on the coast of Syria. An Arab, plowing his field there in 1928, happened to notice that his dog was no longer following him and had in fact disappeared. Retracing his steps, he found that his plow had dislodged a stone in the roof of an underground chamber, and that his dog, sniffing at the hole, had fallen down into ancient Ugarit, once the center of a brilliant civilization which flourished from ca 2000-1600 B.C. Subsequent excavations unearthed hundreds of tablets written in alphabetic cuneiform. Thus the world came to know of an extensive religious literature of Canaan and Syria. Some of the more famous texts are the *Epic of Baal*, the *Legend of Keret*, and the *Tale of Aqhat*.

That Israel was familiar with this literature or the culture that produced it is seen from the many Old Testament parallels to the Ras Shamra tablets. Isaiah's fig-poultice was known in

Ugarit (see 2 Kgs 20:7) as were Baal Zabul and Asherat (1 Kgs 18:19); Lotan, the biblical Leviathan (Is 27:1; Job 26:12); and Dan'el, the sage (see Ezk 14:14; 28:3).

The Lachish Letters (1932)

Lachish, or T. ed-Duweir, was a city in Judah (see Jos 15:39). Lying between Gaza and Hebron, it was not far from Jerusalem. The twenty-one ostraca or letters found here form the only known body of classical Hebrew to be found outside the Bible. They can be dated to 589 B.C., shortly before the fall of Jerusalem. They have unusual philological value and shed light on the time of Jeremiah. One interesting feature is that the name *Yahweh* appears here for only the second time outside the Bible. (The other instance is the Mesha Stone.)

The Khorsabad King List (1932)

At this place, across the river from Mosul and fourteen miles from modern Kuyunjik, there was discovered in 1932 an important list of Assyrian kings. The list makes it possible to establish the line and chronology of the kings with reasonable certitude. One of these great kings, Sargon II (721-705), is mentioned in the Bible (Is 20:1) as the conqueror of Ashdod. The size of his palace gives a better indication of the magnitude of his power and influence.

The Mari Tablets (1933)

Mari (modern T. Hariri), site of the biblical Amorites, was once the brilliant capital city of King Zimri-Lim (1730-1700 B.C.). The royal palace, 250 rooms, with murals and archives, covered fifteen acres. In 1933 some 20,000 clay tablets, along with statues, a temple of Ishtar, a temple tower (or ziggurat) and thirty-two models of the liver (much used in ancient times for divinization) were found there. The tablets provide a considerable amount of information about the civil and political history of the area between 2400-1700 B.C. Mari was destroyed by

Hammurabi in 1696 and lay undisturbed beneath its ruins for almost four millenia!

Nag Hammadi—Chenoboskion (1945)

Chenoboskion, about thirty-two miles north of Luxor in Egypt, yielded thirteen papyrus codices from what was once an ancient monastery. This huge find of Coptic writing dates from the early second to the fourth century A.D. Contained in these pages are many Hermetic and Gnostic works, and public attention has fastened upon one of them, the apocryphal *Gospel of Thomas*, which contains 118 "sayings" of Jesus not found in the canonical gospels. The "sayings" are not notable for their profundity. Borrowings from the Fourth Gospel are rather obvious.

Qumran—The Dead Sea Scrolls (1947)

Perhaps the greatest of all recent archaeological finds in the Near East occurred at Qumran. While looking for some sheep in Wadi Qumran, not far from Ain Feshka at the northwest side of the Dead Sea, Mohammed ed-Din, a young Arab, was diverting himself by throwing stones up the sides of the wadi. One of these random stones made an unusual sound, and the boy, frightened, ran away. The next day he returned with a companion and together they climbed up to the cave. There against the back wall they espied a number of large clay jars, about three feet in height. One of these had been shattered by the unaimed stone. Visions of the fabulous treasures described in *The Arabian Nights* undoubtedly raced through the boys' heads, but what they drew forth from the fragments was something more precious than jewels: a blackened, well-wrapped leather scroll containing the complete text of the prophet Isaiah. The boys brought their find to the local sheikh, who sold it to an antique dealer. After changing hands several times, the scrolls were eventually brought back to Jerusalem, where they are now housed in the magnificent museum built for them by the Israeli government.

The Dead Sea Scrolls, as they have come to be called, are one of the most sensational finds of the twentieth century. Kh. Qumran is known throughout the world. As might be expected, their discovery touched off a frenzied search for other caves; thirty-nine of these have since been explored, yielding copies or fragments of all the Old Testament books (except Esther) in Hebrew, Aramaic, and Greek. Many uncanonical books have also come to light. Along with five copies of the already known apocryphal Book of Jubilees, there were eight of the Book of Enoch. Also discovered were seven copies of a work variously known as the Damascus Covenant or the Zadokite Document. This has many parallels with another document called the *Manual of Discipline*. These documents formed the rule of the Essenes—an intriguing religious community which occupied the site around the time of Christ.

First used in the eighth to seventh century B.C., the site of Qumran was rebuilt under one of the Maccabees, John Hyrcanus (135-104 B.C.) and occupied steadily until the time of Antigonus (40-37). The sudden cessation of coins, 750 of which were found here, point to the abandonment of the site at that time, possibly because of the earthquake which occurred in 31 B.C.

The site was repeopled some thirty years later under Archelaus, son of Herod the Great, who ruled from 4 B.C. to 6 A.D., It was occupied until 68 A.D., when it was destroyed by the Roman soldiers as they closed in on Jerusalem. A military garrison next occupied the site for about thirty years (70-100 A.D.).

With the outbreak of the Second Jewish revolt (132) the site was reoccupied and became the rebels' headquarters. With the failure of the revolt (135 A.D.), Qumran was utterly destroyed, and rested quietly beneath its ruins until 1947.

The Essenes were a sect not mentioned in the Bible but described by Pliny the Elder. They lived according to a *Rule of the Community*, or a *Manual of Discipline (Serek Hayyahad)*. Celibates, they held property in common, lived a common life, and advocated peace, love, and purity. For new members a three-year period of trial, if successful, ended with a ritual bath; after his initiation, the candidate was permitted to eat with the other sectaries. From the presence of a hand-mill among the discoveries it is known that the sectaries were supplied with grain; from the date-pits, that they ate dates; from the coins, that they had some trade; from the tannery, that they had flocks of sheep. An aqueduct, cisterns, a scriptorium, and a cemetery for women as well as men help fill out the picture of life at Qumran.

It has been hazarded that the sectaries hid their scrolls in the Qumran caves shortly before fleeing to Damascus (ca 68 A.D.) to escape the oncoming Romans.

These documents mention a "Teacher of Righteousness" (or "Correct Expositor," or "Right Teacher"), and a "Wicked Priest" who persecuted the Teacher. A giant guessing-game as to the identity of the Right Teacher and Wicked Priest has been going on since the scrolls were first read, but without any great success.

An ever-moot question is the relationship of Jesus and of John the Baptist with Qumran. That there is some connection seems possible; there are too many similarities both in organization and terminology to be ignored. At the same time, radical dissimilarities argue strongly against any close connection between Qumran and Christianity.

Here are some of the similarities in the patterns of life between Qumran and the early Christians. Both lived a communal life, with a common meal, common property, a council of elders, and a system of initiation. Some similar themes can be found in their writings. Both anticipated an eschatological banquet, and both used the theme of light and darkness. The dissimilarities, however, are marked, and there is nothing in the Qumran writings about such characteristically Christian themes as the Incarnation, the Trinity, Jesus' expiatory sacrifice, union with God through the Eucharist, Christ's pre-existence, and original sin. Love for one's neighbor is also conspicuously absent in the scrolls.

All of the Qumran literature has not been published; one estimate is that 95 percent of the contents of Cave Four remain unpublished. What this means is that no definitive conclusions can be drawn about the sect until all the evidence is in. Something, however, can be said, and must be said. It is doubtful that Jesus owed anything to the Essenes. The Dead Sea Scrolls contain little that is original, certainly nothing comparable to Jesus' parables, or other teachings. What similarities there are between his teaching and theirs can be satisfactorily explained by supposing for both a common source, namely, the Old Testament, and, to a lesser degree, the apocrypha of the Old Testament and possibly some early portions of the Talmud.

Gaster, whose book on the scrolls is excellent, sums the matter up by saying that the Scrolls furnish

a picture of the religious and cultural climate in which John the Baptist conducted his mission and in which Jesus was initially reared. They (the Scrolls) portray for us in vivid but authentic colors the environment whose spiritual idiom John and Jesus both spoke, whose concepts they developed and transmuted and whose religious ideas served largely as the seed bed of the New Testament. They also mirror a form of religious organization many elements of which were adopted by the primitive Church. (See Gaster, *The Dead Sea Scriptures*, Doubleday, 1976.)

To say that the Dead Sea Scrolls are the rude clay as yet unmolded by Christian hands, or that Christianity, coming chronologically after the Essenian movement, is a development or effect of that movement is to say too much. Writes Abbé Milik, "Although Essenism bore in itself more than one element that one way or another fertilized the soil from which Christianity was to spring, it is nevertheless evident that the latter religion represents something completely new, which can only be adequately explained by the person of Jesus himself." J.

Jeremias makes the same point: "The literature of Qumran con-firms that nothing comparable (to Jesus' teaching about God's love for sinners) is to be found in contemporary Judaism" *(New Testament Theology,* 121)

Thus ends our brief foray into archaeology. For many a reader it will have been a very liberal kind of education touching upon many areas: ancient history, paleontology, paleography, ceramics (of a kind), geography, chronology, and languages. Hopefully this sortie has also shown the great need for disci-pline in interpretation. The cliché is easy: its only antidote is serious study. The Procrustean Bed beckons enticingly to su-perficial scholars. The books in our bibliogrpahy have nothing in common with such sensational and superficial works as Erich von Daniken's *Chariot of the Gods* which, unfortunately, is about all the "archaeology" some people ever know.

The never-ending exploration of the Negev has produced fragments of several Old Testament books, and some interesting sites like Masada, but little of direct biblical importance. It has yielded nothing to match, say, the Rosetta Stone or the Behistun Inscription. But professional archaeologists live in hope ... ! And even as these pages are being written, word comes of an exciting new find—more than 16,000 clay tablets of an extreme antiquity (ca 2400-2250 B.C.)—at Ebla (modern T. Mardikh) not far from Aleppo in Syria. The language used belongs to the Northwest Semitic and is a sort of paleo-Canaanite; place names abound along with personal names, some of them familiar to readers of the Bible. As these texts are further studied, they should contribute to an understanding of the political and cul-tural situation of the third millenium B.C. (See *The Biblical Ar-chaeologist,* 39:2 May 1976, pp. 44-52.)

TEN

FAITH, REASON, AND THE BIBLE

It is time now to draw together and apply some of the principles touched upon in previous chapters, and to put our knowledge to work to show how faith and reason can work harmoniously together.

We must first point out that faith and reason have not always worked harmoniously. Learned men *do* sometimes doctor the evidence and cook the facts to make them fit beloved theories. Lysenko and his genetics, Cyril Burt and his I.Q.s, the fabricator of the Piltdown Man all come to mind here. Hegel tried to fit all of history into a pattern of thesis, antithesis, and synthesis; but History, that notoriously fickle Dame, laughed at him. Before that it had been the Tübingen School, explaining the Acts as the resolution of a Peter vs. Paul controversy in the early Church, a theory now completely abandoned. Even useful theories have severe limitations. Darwin's theory of natural selection supplied a much-needed framework for countless facts while slighting other important facts: God's part in the process and when, why, and how it all happened. Marx looked upon the world through the prism of economics, and predicted an inevitable class war from which communism would emerge triumphant over capitalism. Marx's vision shows no signs of coming true.

Nor are all examples of fraud and error part of the distant past. Shortly after the Dead Sea Scrolls were discovered in the

1940's, a university professor named John Allegro mistranslated
the Zadokite Scroll, one of the documents, making it appear that
the Teacher of Righteousness mentioned in it was *crucified* by
the Wicked Priest. The teacher and priest were identified as
Jesus and Caiaphas, and Christianity was proclaimed to be a
mere development of the Essene sect. For this example of bad
scholarship, the professor was savagely taken to task by his
peers.

Every theory must stand the crucial test of whether it does
justice to all the facts in the case. To paraphrase an old saying, a
theory is known by the facts it keeps. The more inclusive the
hypothesis, the better its chances of being a sound one.

Almost everyone agrees that the Bible is an important book,
but questions are raised about its accuracy and reliability.
Those who accept the Bible are sometimes disturbed by statements in it which seem to be at variance with facts. One may
close his eyes to such difficulties on the ground that reason has
nothing to do with faith, or one may confront the difficulty
squarely. Although Cardinal Newman once declared that ten
thousand difficulties did not constitute a single doubt, not
everyone is completely at ease with that statement.

The problem of truth and the Bible came up at Vatican II.
Earlier pronouncements had treated the *inerrancy* of the Bible;
Vatican II dropped this unbiblical word to focus upon *the truth
of salvation* which is everywhere clearly proclaimed in the Bible. Things which have nothing to do with salvation do not have
to be defended; if they are wrong, one can simply note their
inaccuracy, also observing that there is nowhere any inaccuracy
or misleading information about God and his plan of salvation.
In other words, the Bible's revelation about God's plan for men
is absolutely reliable. In science, history, and other matters, the
Bible reflects the knowledge of its time.

The Bible and Science

Adam's apple has stuck in many a throat, it has well been
said, and it takes a pillar of salt to digest the story of Jonah and

the whale. But no amount of salt can allay the uneasiness many believers have felt over the murky relationship between the Bible and science. In this realm, the doubts about the truth-value of the Bible have been most intense. The tension between the Bible and science was high during the nineteenth century, and has carried over somewhat into the twentieth century. In order to appreciate the positive and constructive attitude assumed by Vatican II toward this question, the reader is invited to consider a statement of the problem, and then look at some of the less than happy attempts made to resolve it.

The Problem

The scientific problems raised by the Bible, especially by the Old Testament, are many. There is a sun that rises and sets, circling the earth (Tb 2:7; Est 11:11), but it can also be made to halt (Jos 10:12f). The universe and everything in it was created in a period of six days of twenty-four hours each (Gn 1). The earth floats upon the lower waters (Ps 136:6); the upper waters are held in place by the solid dome of the firmament (Gn 1:7; Jb 37:18). The story of Adam and Eve raises the question of evolution; the Flood story, with its Sumerian antecedents, causes many problems. There is the "hare that chews the cud" (Lv 11:6; Dt 14:7). And there are many other questions, as for example the apparent acceptance of a three-decker universe, of Jesus' ascension into heaven, of miracles in general.

These problems are so old and so well known that they scarcely need mentioning. Yet something should be said of them, to acknowledge their existence, and to inform the Bible reader of where he stands.

Concordism as a Solution

Concordism, a modified form of fundamentalism, has as its major premise the assumption that the Bible is actually in basic harmony with modern science, and is perhaps just a step or two ahead of it. At times Moses has been portrayed as the forerunner of Einstein and today's great scientists. He was presumed to have been gifted with special knowledge, such as a notion of how the world was created, and how it was to evolve. If the Bible is read with this in mind, it can be seen to contain truths which modern scientists have only recently been discovering, especially in the fields of geology and biology.

The Genesis account of creation calls for only six days of twenty-four hours each; modern geologists, paleontologists, and astronomers speak casually of the billions of years it took to form the earth, and of the millions of years required for the appearance of human life upon earth. The concordist can try to reconcile this problem by taking the Hebrew word *yom*, which means "day," as meaning a geological era, or eons of time. The theory is sometimes presented in an attractive fashion, but it does seem to be a case of grasping at straws. For one thing, the Bible uses *yom* to mean an ordinary twenty-four hour day; that certainly appears to be the obvious sense of Genesis 1. An even more telling blow at the theory is that the "eons" of Genesis 1 do not match the "eons" of history. The sequence of Genesis 1 is not that of the sciences. The sun, moon, and stars are older than plants, and the fossil remains are not nearly as orderly as the theory would require.

Many serious readers and students of the Bible have become interested in theories advanced by scientists to account for the origins of the universe. The theory which is currently favored by many scientists is called the Big-Bang theory. This suggests that a primordial "cosmic egg" containing all matter long ago exploded violently, producing in the process radioactive protons and electrons. This matter gradually congealed and, under the influence of gravitational forces, the galaxies, stars, and planets formed. All this material in flux might be considered as radiation, in which case the theory appears to provide a new understanding of the biblical command: "Let there be light."

Teilhard de Chardin, a Jesuit scientist, extended the theory of an expanding universe to include organic and cultural evolution. For Teilhard, the universe develops from two competing energies, the "tangential" and the "radial." Tangential energy corresponds to the *Without* of things and is subject to the law of entropy—the fact that the universe is running down. Radial energy corresponds to the *Within* of things and obeys the law of complexification—that is, the "psychic" component of the universe is ever-increasing. For Chardin, primordial matter contained within itself not only consciousness but all the higher manifestations of psychic activity which were destined to appear in the history of the universe. His thinking is cosmic in scope, and accounts for everything, including the Omega Point (God) toward which everything is tending.

Chardin accepted the theories of biogenesis and organic evolution wholeheartedly, and his scientific concordism is the most thoroughgoing ever conceived. He was confident that all theology could and should be made to conform to his insight. However, there are not lacking good scholars who, while acknowledging Chardin's eloquent exposition of his ideas, feel that his theory is neither good science nor good philosophy: some entertain definitely negative views about his whole system.*

Conclusion

In the end, it is unreasonable to imagine that Moses was a super-scientist or that the Bible in other ways anticipated modern science. For Moses, detailed scientific knowledge would have been a decided liability: his hearers would have thought him simply out of his mind if he had expressed such ideas. While they would have accorded him the cautious treatment reserved for the mad (see how David capitalized upon this in 1 Sm 21:13-15), they would never have forsaken the onions and fish and garlic of Egypt (Nm 11:5) to follow him into the desert and freedom.

---

*For example, J. Ratzinger, in his *Theological Highlights of Vatican II* (1966) p. 159.

We can safely say that matters which have no bearing on man's salvation—such as scientific matters—do not affect the truthfulness of the Bible. Its central theme is always God's plan for man's salvation. The so-called "conflict" between Science and the Bible does not exist; the Bible is not a textbook.

Jung remarked in his *Secret of the Golden Flower* that science is the tool of the Western mind. ".With it more doors can be opened than with bare hands. It is part and parcel of our knowledge, and obscures our insight only when it holds that the understanding given by it is the only kind there is." He was right, for there is also the science of salvation, and it pervades the Bible.

The Creation Story

Somewhere between the extremes of utter skepticism and blind faith or gullibility is a respectable middle way of facing the question of science and the Bible. We propose to find this middle way by looking at the Bible's story of creation. We shall recall ancient contexts and look at traditional forms of literary expression to help us determine what the authors of these chapters meant to say. There are a number of side benefits to this quest, not the least of which is the enjoyment of a story well told.

When God made the world (Gn 1), there were no movie cameras or recorders around to capture that event on film or tape. There was in fact nothing at all outside of God himself. The story of how the Supreme Being brought the world into being is itself a creation. Its authors were clever men, even theological geniuses. Immersed in their own world, they produced two remarkable stories of creation in which the dynamic relationship existing between God and his creatures is strikingly brought out.

The first account (Gen 1:1-2:4a) has an almost mathematical structure; the second (Gn. 2:4b-24) is very concrete and visual. Once heard, both stories fix themselves in the memory. Both stories *read* well, and address themselves to the serious question of Who made the universe, and when and why.

Who made the world? God. What is the world? A place for man to live in. When was it made? In the beginning. Why was it made? To show that God is good, and very much interested in man. These are answers a man can live by.

The story of creation (Gn 1) occupies seven days or one week, and within this familiar framework the creation of all things is distributed in a way that has aroused the admiration of the ages. *In the beginning,* when God made the heavens and the earth, the earth was a *tohu wabohu,* a formless wasteland. (The very sound of these Hebrew syllables suggests chaos and confusion.) Moreover, darkness prevailed over the deep, and God's spirit hovered over the water. What next? Well, no one in his right mind works in the dark; one must have light to see. Logically, the first thing God does is to "turn on the lights." So we read: "Let there be light. And there was light." God called this beautiful creation "day," the darkness "night."

The next task was to manage the *tohu wabohu,* to separate and control the waters of the deep. To do this God simply said "Let there be a vault . . . to divide the waters in two." And so it was done. Space was provided for the waters: one above the vault or firmament, and another for the waters under the vault. This was the work of the second day.

On the third day two things were created. The waters were gathered together and dry land appeared, and God gave them the names of seas and earth. On this day also, God commanded the earth to produce vegetation—seed-bearing plants and fruit trees. As before, all was done immediately and exactly as he commanded it to be. Running through the account is the notion of God's extraordinary power. Whatever he does, he does effortlessly, with the greatest of ease. And everything turns out well.

But there is an unexpected turn to the story. Instead of simply continuing the inventory of things created, day after day, the authors hit upon the remarkable idea of making the last three days parallel the first three. The "ordering" of the universe (days 1-2-3) is followed by the work of "decorating" the universe (4-5-6).

On the fourth day, God created the sun, the moon, and the stars, making them to "decorate" the light that he made on the first day. How marvellously done, and how profound a teaching. The Israelites were surrounded by people who worshiped the sun (Egypt), or the moon (Babylon), or the stars (Assyria). To the Israelite, the sun and moon and stars, gods to his neighbors, are nothing more than creations of the Almighty, who brought them into being by a simple command. He set them to govern the day and the night, to divide light from darkness. They were creations, not gods to be worshiped.

In our own times, the work of the fourth day broke unexpectedly into a famous debate during the Scopes Trial between two famous men: Clarence Darrow, the truculent iconoclast, and William Jennings Bryan, the silver-tongued orator. Knowing Bryan to be a staunch fundamentalist, Darrow drew him into an affirmation that the Bible was everywhere literally true, and then confronted him with the question: "How could light have been created before the sun?" Caught in the trap, Bryan could not answer. Darrow's question would never have disturbed an Israelite who knew nothing and cared little about the nature of the sun. He knew that on cloudy days when the sun was invisible, there was always daytime followed by night. That was enough for him.

On the fifth day, God graced the upper firmament with birds and all flying things, and decorated the seas with fish. On the sixth day, corresponding to day three, God adorned the dry land with the animals and every kind of living creature. Then, in his own image, God made man. After that, God rested from his work of creation: it was the seventh day.

At the end of each day's work, God saw that what he had made was *good*. After the creation of man, God saw that all he had made was *very good*. Thus with a simple statement, the Bible has cut the ground from under any attempt to say that things are evil in themselves. God, himself all good, could not make anything that was not good. Nor did he need practice, or show signs of improvement in his creative ability. Whatever he made came into being exactly as he intended it to be.

Here, schematically, it is a resume of Gn 1, 1-2, 4:

ORDER			DECOR	
Day	Creation	Day		Creation
1	Light	4		Sun, moon, stars
2	Firmament	5		Birds and fish
3	Dry land	6		Animals
	Vegetation			Man

7 Rest

Thomas Aquinas, the Angelic Doctor, following his predecessor St. Augustine and his teacher Albert the Great, was greatly concerned lest the teaching of the faith be presented in such a way as to arouse the scorn or derision of unbelievers. It should always be intellectually credible, he said. Aquinas taught that creation in Gn 1 was not to be taken chronologically, but should be rather recognized as a systematic or *logical* device used for the purpose of teaching.

The Biblical Universe

Guided only by the naked eye and the words of Scripture, ancient peoples worked out a logical view of the world which, however erroneous, does them no little credit. Here is a brief summary of this world view which will help the reader understand many passages of the Bible.

First of all, the heavens look like an inverted bowl. Not only that, they look *solid.* The stars all seem to be the same distance away, some brighter than others, but all fixed in the solid vault. The stars maintain the same relative positions in the sky as they march across the night, but the sun, moon, and planets play hide and seek in the sky. Like the clouds, they move about er-

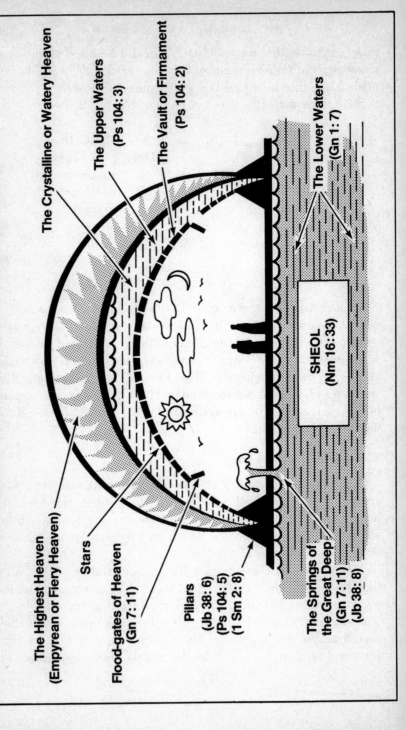

THE HEBREW CONCEPTION OF THE UNIVERSE

The Crystalline or Watery Heaven

The Upper Waters (Ps 104:3)

The Vault or Firmament (Ps 104:2)

The Lower Waters (Gn 1:7)

SHEOL (Nm 16:33)

The Highest Heaven (Empyrean or Fiery Heaven)

Stars

Flood-gates of Heaven (Gn 7:11)

Pillars
(Jb 38:6)
(Ps 104:5)
(1 Sm 2:8)

The Springs of the Great Deep
(Gn 7:11)
(Jb 38:8)

ratically beneath the solid firmament. Since the number of planets known to the ancients was eight, one sometimes encounters references to the "harmony of the universe."

For the inhabitants of the Fertile Crescent, rain was a matter of life and death. Observing that rain always came down from above, they concluded that a heavenly reservoir or store of water existed *above the firmament:* in the Bible these are the "upper waters," and the heaven that contained them was called the "watery" or "crystalline" heaven. But ancient man noted that springs and rivers welled *up* from the earth as well. Thus, they not irrationally concluded that there had to be "lower waters" as well. Read now the story of the Flood in Gn 7. "The sluices of heaven" (i.e., the star-openings) were opened, and it rained forty days and forty nights. And "the springs of the great deep" broke through the earth. As the waters burst the barriers set them by God (Gn 1:7), chaos once more prevailed.

Next, to explain why the stars twinkled, the ancients reasoned that there had to be a fiery or empyrean heaven above the crystalline or watery heaven. It made sense. It is the nature of fire to flicker and flare, and the twinkling of the stars was fire seen through the clear heavenly waters.

Such views had a very long life, appearing in apocalyptic literature and as late as Dante's *Divine Comedy.* They seem naive and fanciful to us who know much more about the heavens. But the old views made a kind of sense. We rightly marvel at the thought of a universe suspended in space and held together by mysterious forces of gravity, but centuries ago the Israelites pictured a God-made world that floated upon the waters of the great deep!

For them, as for us, the world was worthy of respect and reverence.

The Bible and History

The patriarch Jacob wrestled with an angel throughout a long night, and would not let it go until it blessed him (Gn 32).

The Church has been wrestling with the problem of history and the Bible for centuries. It has been a long night, but with the advent of two great biblical documents, the *Divino Afflante* and the *Dei Verbum*, the dawn seems finally to have arrived.

Bible history is concerned with God's plan for man's salvation, and the Bible is its own witness. That is, the Bible itself is the oldest and the closest "evidence" for what it contains. The natural question to ask, then, is "How much of it is true?" The answer to this will depend on one's idea of history.*

Does history really consist in holding a mirror up to the past and "telling it like it was?" History deals with the past and attempts to preserve it in a concrete way, but written history never tells it like it was, for the simple reason that the historian himself is part of the story. He chooses the facts he relates, and interprets them in the retelling. Behind his selectivity lie factors which influenced his literary activity—namely, his purpose and his religious outlook. His purpose may not have been to write literal history.

History is a jewel with a thousand faces, and Bible history is in a class by itself: clever, sophisticated, creative, often poetic, almost always entertaining and instructive. At times it sounds like folklore, reflecting local traditions and memories. It can be lofty but is also very earthy. Above all, Bible history is profoundly religious. As Toynbee has said: "History is a vision ... of God revealing himself in action to souls that were sincerely seeking him."

Before discussing the biblical conception of history, let us examine the Bible's handling of the data of history. In particular, we will see how the writers of the Bible viewed time and numbers.

The Bible and Time

When one takes up the Bible and reads the first line, "In the beginning ... " he might understandably assume that he is

---

*It should perhaps be stressed here again that there are many different literary genres besides history in the Bible.

about to read an orderly account with a beginning and an end. In a sense that assumption is correct, although what is in between is by no means easily "ordered" or located in time. The Bible seems to speak clearly enough about time, and once an Anglican bishop named Ussher (1581-1656) tried to draw up a biblical chronology. His method was to add up all the Old Testament references to time—the ages of Adam and the Patriarchs, the years of kings' reigns, etc.—to determine the date of the creation. His conclusion was that the world had been created 4004 years before Christ. This bit of information found its way into many Bibles in the form of a footnote to Gn 1: *In the beginning*—B.C. 4004; A.M. 1 (*Anno Mundi* or Year of the World, one).

As biblical science progressed, however, the "house" of Ussher was doomed to fall. The ages of the patriarchs who lived before and after the Flood (Gn 5 and 11) have never failed to astound the modern reader. Did Adam really live to be 930 years old, and Methusaleh 969? Did God prolong life in those early days so that the earth could be populated? It seems quite unlikely that God would multiply that kind of miracle. But what then is the explanation that will satisfy our inquisitive minds?

Writers of other ancient histories are known to have assigned great ages to their ancestors. The Assyrian annalists drew up king-lists of monarchs who lived from 10,000 to 20,000 years! Here, as in the Bible, a literary convention was at work. The authors of the biblical genealogies (Gn 5 and 11) were trying to bridge the gap between their own day and ancient times. They were looking for a way to give history some continuity, and to show that God is the Lord of all history. It was not an easy thing to do. Tradition had supplied these writers with a mere handful of names, and few, few facts. They "spread" these precious names and facts by assigning great ages to the patriarchs; thus they were able to span the vast stretches of time betwen themselves and the beginnings. This idea smacks of genius. The ages of the patriarchs get shorter as they come closer to the writer's time (with an occasional bounce upward to give the account some life). Finally the writer makes the connection with his own time. It was up to the reader to understand that the biblical authors did not really know how old the patriarchs were, but that they lived a long time ago, and yet belonged to the human race.

Another difficulty for Ussher was the fact that the years assigned to the kings of Judah and Israel have no fixed point of reference; everything is up in the air, so to speak. Ahaz began to reign in the seventeenth year of Pekah, who became king in the fifty-second year of Azariah! The dates sound precise, but they really are not.

The New Testament is much closer to us in time, but there are problems. Despite Luke's list of historical personages (3:1ff), it is difficult to determine just when Jesus was born. It was certainly before 4 B.C., when Herod the Great, slayer of infants, died. But a more precise date involves much speculation. We would also need to speculate about the time of year of Jesus' birth. Before Pope Liberius, the feast of Jesus' birth had been variously celebrated on March 21-25, 28, April 13-19, and May 29. Pope Liberius chose December 25 as the feast to provide Christians with an alternative to the pagan feast of the Sol Invictus (The Unconquered Sun), annually observed during the winter solstice. A plausible date for Jesus' birth might be worked out on the basis of Augustus' decree calling for a world-wide census. The Jews hated any census (see 2 Sm 24), and the Romans did not needlessly antagonize their subject peoples. So if a census had been set for the fall of the year, a time when the harvest was in and the rainy season (December-March) had not yet begun, the inconvenience of travelling to one's ancestral village would have been somewhat reduced. Jesus then may possibly have been born sometime in the fall— say, October or November.

Another question arises concerning Jesus' age and the date of his death. Luke noted (3:23) that Jesus began to preach when he was about thirty years old. If he was born ca 6-7 B.C., as seems certain, and began his public ministry late in the year 27 or early in 28 A.D., as also seems indicated, he would already have been in his mid-thirties, with two (or three) more years of life before his crucifixion. Informed opinion sets the date of his death as April 7, 30 A.D., or April 3, 33 A.D. and of the two dates, the first is preferred.

In fact, our whole modern concern for exactitude is clearly not biblical. Clement of Alexandria (d. 215) had some harsh things to say about people who wanted to know when people were born; what mattered was how and when a man died, for that was when martyrs showed the stuff they were made of, and entered into heavenly happiness. Reflecting this attitude, the liturgy of the Church celebrates the death dates, rather than the birthdays, of saints and martyrs.

Where time is concerned, then, the Bible tells us little, other than that there is a time for everything (Qoh 3:1-8). Time is under the control of God who appoints the time or the hour for things to happen. The hour of man's salvation has sounded, and we are living in the end-time. At the appointed time, judgment too will arrive on schedule.

The Numbers in the Bible

Biblical authors were not obsessed with the idea of exact expression. What drove them was the desire to communicate their views about God and themselves and the world. Moved by the Spirit to do this, they used whatever materials they had in a creative way and were not afraid to embellish a story. Here are a few examples.

Gideon assembled an army of 32,000 men; then, reducing it to 300 (Jgs 7) he won a smashing victory. At the Jordan River 42,000 Ephraimites were slain because they said "Sibboleth" instead of "Shibboleth," their accent betraying their disloyalties (Jgs 12:6).

Samson slew a thousand Philistines with "the jawbone of an ass" (Jgs 15:15). The Israelites slew 25,100 men of Benjamin, all of them swordsmen (Jgs 20:35). The women sang, "Saul has slain his thousands and David his ten thousands" (1 Sm 18:7).

It seems fairly clear that these military exploits are somewhat exaggerated (see pp. 109-112). But what would a story-teller be without exaggeration? For example, I heard a modern Arab confide to a friend that there had been two or three hundred people at his house on a weekend. It was pointed out to him that his house could hold at most fifty or sixty people. "As I said," he replied, "very many people came."

One must of course be careful not to over-simplify the problems that arise while reading the Bible. Neither should one magnify them unduly. The numbers given in the Bible give us some idea of what happened, and from them one can judge whether a matter was important or not. But above all, the mind of the author and his purpose should be paramount. Each case must obviously be considered by itself.

The Old Testament and History

In the *Méthode historique,* written at the turn of the century, P. Lagrange worked out a simple rule of thumb for classifying Old Testament history. There was *edifying history,* as in Tobit and Jonah, wherein some truth was skillfully conveyed to the reader; *objective history,* wherein fact predominated; and the *history of origins,* a special classification for Gn 1-11. Lagrange argued that in biblical history there is always a feel for reality which at times went beyond mere fact, and that some striking reality always loomed in the background, such as the ziggurat or artificial mountain in the story of the Tower of Babel. Always too, the religious significance of what was related was of greater importance than the actual history, and it is under that aspect that we should seek the author's point.

About the same time, the scholar Von Hummelauer identified eight different literary forms in the Old Testament, each distinguished from the others by its distance from historical fact. They were: religious history, ancient history, historical epic, popular tradition or folklore, idealized history, midrash, parable, and fable. That such distinctions sound familiar today is an indication of how far biblical studies have progressed since then.

But biblical history is no run-of-the-mill history. Take for example the threefold account of the death of Antiochus Epiphanes. This archenemy of the Jews is said to have died in bed, was cut to pieces, and died of an intestinal disorder (see 1 Mc 6:8-16; 2 Mc 1:13-16; 9:5-28). What is the reader to make of this kind of reporting? Probably the ancient scribe, finding three different versions in circulation, used them all. He trusted that his readers would know that while the fact of Antiochus' death was widely vouched for, the details were not.

There are a number of other intriguing things about the Old Testament that call for attention. The pages of its historical books are sprinkled with conversations and speeches, some of them of a very high caliber. But—what did God really say at creation (Gn 1-2), and do we have his words to Adam and Eve (Gn 3)?

The book of Deuteronomy contains a series of eloquent discourses of Moses, verbatim accounts, it would seem; it is Moses' testament to his people before he died. However, it is unlikely that these are actually verbatim accounts of Moses' speeches. The ancients had a much more casual attitude toward historical exactitude than we do. In Homer, for example, war-like speeches followed a convention. They were clearly designed to stir up soldierly valor by describing the sweet taste of victory and promising abundant spoils. The motives for the war in progress were recalled to memory to stir up the proper mental attitude toward one's enemy. But who knew exactly what was said at Ilium? Homer used what information he had and, while reworking it, constructed those speeches which suited the occasion and were reasonably close to what must have been said. In all this, the modern reader can appreciate the poet's creative skill. That was the way, the only way, ancient speeches could be written. Thucydides, Herodotus, and others followed the same pattern and it is not unreasonable to suppose the men who wrote the Bible did so too. Moreover, the historical books were worked over and brought up to date periodically, under God's guidance and inspiration.

The composite character of many Old Testament books is a relatively recent discovery, and one that underscores the originality of the Bible. For us, authorship is a simple matter; one writes or dictates and publishes a book. We are familiar also with ghost writers whose writings are put out under another's name. But in ancient times, a much looser notion prevailed. Books were put out under the name of one who was a recognized master in that field. Thus the Psalms were called the Psalms of David; the book of Wisdom was entitled the Wisdom of Solomon. The attribution of these works to David and Solomon would guarantee that the writings which were offered under the patronage of such great wise men would be given a respectful hearing. The principle at work here is that of *pseudonymity*, and in time this meant that a literature of unknown authorship came into being. The followers of great masters, dedicated to the master's spirit and pursuing his thought amid new situations, did not hesitate to add to his writings. Deutero-Isaiah (40-66) is probably an instance of this. In any case, the ideas of authorship and of history, seen through Semitic eyes, are not always quite what we mean by the same terms.

Before turning to the New Testament and History, a word about a surprising element in the Old Testament—namely, myth and mythology.

Myth, Mythology, and Bible

Few words so instantly raise a believer's defenses as the word "myth" or "mythology" when used in connection with the Bible. "What accord is there between Christ and Belial?"

Ancient man peopled the world with mysterious and unpredictable forces, with gods and goddesses. In the literary form called myth, he attempted to deal with the reality that lay beyond the mere observation of nature. We call that transcendental reality which in some mysterious way affects man and his world "the divine." How this realm related to man and his condition, and man to it, was the concern of the myth-makers. Myth at its best was a symbolic expression of truth, a way of coping with the problem of cosmic and human origins.

Myth-making is a serious business, a groping after truth, and it is perhaps only to be expected that traces of this respectable literary form should crop up in the Bible. Allusions to mythological forces appear most often in the poetic books. These are not so much evidences of belief—the Israelite scribes again and again extolled the exclusive greatness of their God—as of the fact that the scribes were men of their times, and were acquainted with other literatures. A writer today might casually refer to the Big Bad Wolf, or to Little Red Riding Hood or Paul Bunyan. He would certainly be indignant if anyone were to accuse him of believing in mythology or folklore.

Here are some of the passing references to mythological beings which can be found in the Bible. The reader may want to supplement these remarks with the articles on myth and mythology found in the *New Catholic Encyclopedia* and elsewhere.

Job (3:8) refers to *Leviathan*, also called the Dragon or the fleeing, twisting Serpent. This monster of primeval chaos also appears in the Ras Shamra texts. *Tiamat* or the *Sea* (7:12) is mentioned in the Babylonian cosmogonies. Yahweh, however, was the one who established order out of *Chaos*, and ever after held the Sea and its monsters in control. *Rahab* (9:13) was another name for primeval Chaos. *Lilith* was a female demon (Is 34:14; Jb 18:15), and various other assorted ghoulies and ghosties, satyrs and desert-demons are mentioned. (The *Jerusalem Bible* provides good footnotes on these, as does the *Jerome Biblical Commentary*, #77:23-31.) However, there is never any question that these creatures are all vastly inferior to the Lord, the maker of heaven and earth and all things.

Gn 1-11 is usually called proto-history. It would be misleading to say that these chapters, which deal with the origins of things, contain no history in the modern sense of the term. This would suggest that they are not history at all. Actually, Gn 1-11 relates, in simple and figurative language adapted to the understanding of a less developed people, the fundamental truths presupposed for the economy of salvation, along with the popular description of the origin of the human race, and of the Chosen People.

In any case, the point is subtly made again and again in the Bible—and often not so subtly but with crushing directness—that the "forces" which other peoples worshiped were mere creatures of Yahweh, the one and only God of heaven and earth.

To conclude: some biblical thought and language is mythical, but instead of this casting doubt upon its historical reality, it simply points up the fact that symbolic expression leaves something to be desired.

The Gospels and History

The Old Testament has no monopoly on problems. During the past 200 years the New Testament has also been a battleground. Nothing—from the Infancy narratives to Jesus' life, death, and resurrection—has gone unchallenged. Both historical and literary critics have exercised their skills on the New Testament. What is left of the poor gospels? Has the new knowledge left us any the wiser?

During the course of Vatican II, the Pontifical Biblical Commission issued a document on the historical truth of the gospels which was endorsed by the Council and worked into the *Dei Verbum*. What follows here is a summary of a most enlightening document. The principles contained in it are like beacons of guiding light for the Bible reader.

The Council goes on record by reaffirming the traditional view of the gospels: they are held to be of apostolic origin. The wording is significant. All four gospels are *held to be* of apostolic origin. The Council did *not* say that they are *believed to be* of apostolic origin. History is thus accorded its right to speak in this matter. Moreover, the term "origin" is wider than that of authorship. Non-members of the Twelve—Mark, Luke, John's disciples, and others—played an active part in the composition of the gospels. The four gospels "reliably" hand on the events of Jesus' human life, that is, his deeds and teachings. The word "reliably" is preferred to Bultmann's "creatively." This influential scholar spoke ambiguously of a "creative community," but the creativity of the community can be questioned. Moreover, Bultmann's terms *Historie* (the plain fact) and *Geschichte* (what the fact means to me) are far from being clear, and suggest that the gospels are basically non-historical and unreliable.

Understanding of the Good News was won by stages. After a thing has happened, things become clearer. The Good News announced by Jesus, however welcome to mankind, was almost too good to be true. It took time for men to get used to the idea and to grasp what had happened and what it meant. First Jesus' public ministry, what he did and said, had been incredibly exciting. No man ever spoke like this man, people said. Unfortunately, death put an end to his stirring words. Then to everyone's astonishment, he rose from the dead. The apostles were finally fully convinced of Jesus' divinity, and went everywhere preaching the resurrection. They spoke of Jesus in various ways, recalling his teachings and his parables and incidents of his life. The believing community soon possessed hymns, doxologies, and prayers. All of this constituted the second phase of the Good News. The third phase saw the composition of the written gospel, based upon the pool of oral and written sources which by now clustered about the name of Jesus.

The gospel writers used this material as authors the world over use theirs; they sometimes synthesized what Jesus said and did, or sometimes expanded it, explaining the meaning of Jesus' words as the needs of their communities demanded. Similar materials were gathered together. For example, the Sermon on the Mount in Matthew contains teachings scattered about in Luke's Gospel. Or, in Mark 10:28-30, the word *father* is omitted, while the word *wife* is added in the parallel passage (Lk 18:29). Mt 5:32 contains what may be an addition ("except in the case of fornication"); and Mt 28:19 sets forth a baptism in the name of the Father, Son, and Holy Spirit, quite certainly a step in depth beyond baptism in the name of Jesus.

The gospels abound in places where the evangelists have

changed the order of events, or even of Jesus' words. Chronology for them was of little importance, or at any rate other purposes were more important. The evangelists do not usually put things in chronological order. To the ordinary layman, such "modern" statements may seem to strike at the heart of everything sacred, but in fact, we have known this almost from the beginning. Centuries ago, St. Augustine noticed the free way Matthew handled his materials, and how the materials were reworked and used in different contexts. Catholic scholars like Lagrange were saying these same things at the turn of the present century, and the Biblical Commission's 1964 document, in a very real sense a traditional document, repeated them. To put it in a nutshell: the sacred authors proclaimed the honest truth about Jesus Christ. Their adaptations may have affected the sequence of the gospel story, but not its truth.

Thus, as the *Dei Verbum* says, the gospels reliably hand on to us the deeds and teachings of Jesus. The New Testament is based on historical fact, and is the proclamation of that fact. It richly rewards all who study it and follow its teachings.

EPILOGUE

The more one studies God's word, the more he comes to realize that he is dealing with a book that has been studied and loved by the greatest minds in Christianity. It is a humbling discovery, but at the same time one that is reassuring. The Bible is good for us.

During the public ministry, Jesus moved about surrounded by people. Among them there was, on one occasion, an ailing woman who said to herself, "If I can but touch his clothes, I shall get well" (Mk 5:28). When she succeeded in doing just that, she was healed. On another occasion some Greeks said to Philip, "Sir, we should like to see Jesus" (Jn 12:22), and when some disciples asked Jesus where he lived, he gave them an enigmatic answer that echoes still: "Come and see" (Jn 1:39).

One can approach Jesus, not in a physical, spatial way, but through a knowledge and love which are fostered by reading the word of God. St. Jerome said it well when he wrote: "Ignorance of the Scriptures is ignorance of Christ."

We meet God through Jesus Christ, in the sacred writings. Sometimes, as we read them, we find that our hearts too are burning (Lk 24:32). And this can happen more and more frequently, as we move away from many of our para-liturgical practices and, following the invitation of Vatican II, make the Scriptures more and more a part of our life.

These introductory pages, dealing with history, languages, dates, textual criticism, and theology, are but the touching of the hem of Jesus' garments. There remains listening and responding to God as he speaks to us in the depths of our being. We would do well to pay heed to Jeremiah's advice,

Let not the wise man boast of his wisdom
nor the valiant of his valor,
nor the rich man of his riches.
But if any man would boast,
let him boast of this,
of understanding and knowing me (Jer 9:23).

The Latins used to conclude their works with the phrase *Finis libri, sed non finis quaerendi,* that is, "This book ends, but not the quest." Somehow the words seem fitting here, for as Isaiah has said,

The grass withers, the flower fades,
But the word of our God remains forever (Is 40:8).

BIBLIOGRAPHY

It is impossible to keep a bibliography up to date. Listed in this one are books usually available. Some standard works which are widely known are listed even though they are out of print.

Archaeology

Albright, W. F. *The Archaeology of Palestine* (Pelican pb, 1961)

Archaeology (Keter, 1974). Brief accounts of recent activities; excerpted from the new Jewish Encyclopedia.

The Biblical Archaeologist (Cambridge, 1938-). Articles aimed at acquainting readers with recent work in the field.

The Biblical Archaeologist Reader (Anchor, 1961-64) is edited by G. E. Wright and D. N. Freedman.

Ceram, C. *Gods, Graves, and Scholars* (Knopf pb, 1960). An engaging account of recent and older discoveries of interest.

Pritchard, J. B. *Ancient Near Eastern Texts: An Anthology of Texts and Pictures,* with Supplement. 3rd ed. 1969. Vol. II: *A New Anthology of Texts and Pictures* (Princeton University Press, 1973). Pb.

Wright, G. E. *Biblical Archaeology* (Westminster, 1963). An abbreviated introduction of the author's larger work.

Reference Works

Albright, W. F. *From the Stone Age to Christianity* (Doubleday pb, 1957). A remarkable synthesis by a scholar of outstanding erudition and archaeological expertise.

Anderson, B. W. *Understanding the Old Testament* (3rd ed.) (Prentice-Hall, 1975). Simply excellent.

Baly, D. *A Geography of the Bible.* (Harper and Row, 1974). Revised edition of a valuable work.

De Vaux, Roland. *Ancient Israel* (McGraw pb, 1965). A classic work on the life and social institutions of Israel, written by the former director of the Ecole Biblique.

Grollenberg, L. H. *Atlas of the Bible* (Nelson, 1956). A first-rate work with excellent illustrations, maps, and text.

May, H., Hung, G., and Hamilton, R. (eds.) *Oxford Bible Atlas* (rev. ed. 1974).

Dictionaries

Kittel, R. *Theological Dictionary of the New Testament* (Eerdmans, 1971). A scholarly achievement, but somewhat too exhaustive.

Léon-Dufour, X. *Dictionary of Biblical Theology* (Seabury, 1973). A well-presented reference work.

Richardson, A. *A Dictionary of Christian Theology.* (Westminster, 1969). Clear, balanced, and modern.

Concordances

Hartdegen, S. (ed.) *Nelson's Complete Concordance of the New American Bible.* (1977). A welcome arrival. Entries from the whole Bible, in alphabetical order.

Jeanne d'Arc, Sister (ed.). *Modern Concordance to the New Testament* (Doubleday, 1976). A superlative work, soon to be joined by its Old Testament counterpart.

Histories of Israel

Bright, John. *A History of Israel.* 2nd ed. (Westminster, 1972). Conservative, readable.

De Vaux, R. *Early History of Israel* (Westminster, 1977). Brilliant first half of a project interrupted by the author's untimely death.

Finegan, Jack. *Light From the Ancient Past.* 2nd ed. (Princeton, 1959). A book well worth having. Tells of ancient history as it touches on the Bible. Many illustrations.

Noth, M. *The History of Israel.* 2nd ed. (Adam and Black, 1960). Influential work by a leading scholar. His "Israelite amphictyony" has recently come under heavy attack.

Introductions

Fohrer, G. *Introduction to the Old Testament* (10th ed.) (Abingdon, 1968).

Kaiser, O. *Introduction to the Old Testament* (Augsburg pb, 1977).

Marxsen, W. *Introduction to the New Testament* (Fortress pb, 1976). A "special" Introduction.

Spivery-Smith, *Anatomy of the New Testament* (Macmillan, 1974). A standard textbook, fairly readable and containing much information.

Commentaries

One-Volume

Brown, Fitzmyer, Murphy (eds) *The Jerome Biblical Commentary* (Prentice, 1968). A one-volume work by members of the Catholic Biblical Association. A library in itself. Has commentaries on each of the books of the Bible plus excellent topical articles.

Peake's *Commentary on the Bible* (Black, Rowley, eds.) (Nelson, 1952). Fully revised and a standard work.

Multi-Volume

Anchor Bible. Doubleday's ambitious project of a modern scientific commentary by Protestant, Catholic, and Jewish authors on all books of the Bible. From 1964 on.

Cambridge Bible Commentaries on the New English Bible. This scholarly series, begun in 1966, replaces the excellent older series.

Hermeneia. Fortress began this series in 1973. Serious commentaries on the Bible.

Interpreter's Dictionary of the Bible, with Supplement. Five volumes of highly informative articles. (Abingdon, 1962-76).

Journey: Guided Study Programs in the Catholic Faith. An impressive, realistic work by a competent guide, Father Marcel Gervais, who directs the Divine Word Centre of Religious Education (260 Colborne St., London, Ont. Canada).

Tyndale: New Testament Commentaries (ed. R. V. G. Tasker) (Eerdmans, 1975). An excellent, well-written series of twenty volumes (pb). Highly informative, sticking closely to the text and occasionally impatient with some Roman Catholic positions.

Pentateuch

Vawter, B. *A Path Through Genesis* (Sheed & Ward, 1956).

_____ *On Genesis: A New Reading* (Doubleday, 1977). An impressive, up-to-date commentary by a scholar who writes well.

Von Rad, G. *Genesis.* Revised ed. (Westminster, 1963). Scholarly work by a noted German biblical writer. Not for the faint-hearted!

Old Testament Prophets

Heaton, E. W. *The Old Testament Prophets* (Rev. ed., Darton, 1977). Addressed to the student and general reader.

Lindblom, J. *Prophecy in Ancient Israel* (Fortress, 1972). A serious contribution from a Swedish scholar.

Scott, R. B. Y. *The Relevance of the Prophets.* (Rev. ed. Macmillan, 1968). Excellent and readable.

Vawter, B. *The Conscience of Israel* (Andrews & McMeel, 1973). Helpful toward understanding the prophets and their works.

Von Rad, G. *The Message of the Prophets* (Harper pb, 1972).

Old Testament Writings

Lewis, C. S. *Reflections on the Psalms* (Harcourt pb, 1964). Stimulating insights by a well-known author.

Mowinckel, S. *Psalms in Israel's Worship* (Abingdon, 1962). The author is one of the pioneers in applying form-critical principles to the study of the psalms.

Scott, R. B. Y. *The Way of Wisdom* (Macmillan, 1971). A useful and fairly popular introduction to the wisdom literature.

Biblical Theology

Eichrodt, W. *Theology of the Old Testament* (Westminster, 1974). Of proven worth.

Gelin, A. *Key Concepts of the Old Testament* (Paulist pb, 1963). For the initiated; instructive.

Jacob, E. *Theology of the Old Testament* (Harper pb, 1975). Concentrates on the great themes.

Jeremias, J. *New Testament Theology* (Scribner, 1971). One of the important books written on the New Testament in the last fifty years.

McKenzie, J. L. *A Theology of the Old Testament* (Doubleday pb, 1976). Distinctive approach to a controversial subject. Clear, vigorous style.

Von Rad, G. *Old Testament Theology* (Harper, 1965). The author's name is itself a recommendation.

General Works

Brown, R. E. *New Testament Essays* (Doubleday, 1965). Fourteen essays on critical issues.

——— *Peter in the New Testament.* A Collaborative Assessment by Protestant and Roman Catholic Scholars (Augsburg, 1973). A judicious report on the important debate on papal primacy.

——— *The Virginal Conception and Bodily Resurrection of Jesus* (Paulist, 1973). Good treatment of a number of controversial topics. As usual, the author is "where the action is."

——— *The Birth of the Messiah* (Doubleday, 1977). A serious scholarly work that "defends" the Christmas story from the scorn of experts and the sentimentality of the naive.

Charlier, C. *Christian Approach to the Bible* (Westminster, 1967). Literate and readable.

Dodd, C. H. *The Founder of Christianity* (Collins, 1971). Crisp distillation of the author's lifetime of New Testament study.

Dulles, A. *Apologetics and the Biblical Christ* (Newman, 1964). Clear expression of the real problems that arise from the New Testament, and from traditional views about Jesus.

Fuller, R. H. *The New Testament in Current Study* (Scribner, 1976). Good, but hard going.

Harrington, W. *Key to the Bible*. Three volumes (Alba, 1975). Paperback edition of the author's General Introduction.

Lagrange, M. J. *The Gospel of Jesus Christ* (Newman, 1958). The gospels speak for themselves. One of the great works of our century.

Martin, G. *Reading Scripture as the Word of God* (Servant Books, 1975). A clear and practical guide for Bible readers.

McKenzie, J. L. *Vital Concepts of the Bible* (Dimension, 1969). Reprints.

Morton, H. V. *In the Footsteps of the Master ... In the Steps of St. Paul ...* and *Through Lands of the Bible* (1935ff). Morton is an engaging companion for a trip to the Near East. Pleasant anecdotes and historical information painlessly administered.

Neill, S. *The Interpretation of the Bible 1861-1961.* (Oxford, 1964). A charming and intelligent book about biblical wars of the past 100 years.

———— *Jesus Through Many Eyes—An Introduction ...* (Fortress, 1976)

New Testament: General Works

Pope, H. *English Versions of the Bible* (Greenwood, revised ed., 1952). Well-documented history of how the Bible came to be put into English.

Robinson, J. A. T. *Can We Trust the New Testament?* (Eerdmans, 1977). This pb says: Yes, yes, yes!

Smalley, B. *Study of the Bible in the Middle Ages* (Notre Dame pb, 1964). A good study of a much-neglected era.

Vogrimler, J. (ed.). *Commentary on the Documents of Vatican II* (Seabury, 1967-69). An excellent cooperative record of the evolution of the documents.

Wright, G. E. *God Who Acts* (Allenson pb, 1952). God reveals himself through his actions in history.

Intertestamental Literature

Charles, R. H. *The Apocrypha and Pseudepigrapha of the Old Testament* (Oxford, 1913). An exhaustive treatment (texts and notes), in two volumes.

James, M. R. *The Old Testament Legends (and) The Apocryphal New Testament* (Oxford, 1963).

Hennecke, E. *New Testament Apocrypha* (Westminster, 2 Vol. 1963-65)

Metzger, B. M. *Introduction to the Apocrypha.* (Oxford, 1957)
────── *Oxford Annotated Apocrypha: Revised Standard Version* (Oxford, 1977)

Textual Criticism

Aland, K. et al. *The Greek New Testament* (United Bible Societies, 1976, 3rd edition). Critical text of the New Testament, including a dictionary. Intended for translators.

Finegan, Jack. *Encountering Biblical Manuscripts* (Eerdmans, 1974). Actually deals with texts, especially the papyri. For the student who knows some Greek.

Grant, Robert. *A Historical Introduction to the New Testament: Textual Criticism* (Touchstone pb, 1972). A clear, informative account of textual procedures.

Greenlee, J. H. *Introduction to New Testament Textual Criticism.* (Eerdmans pb, 1975).

Kenyon, Sir Frederic. *Our Bible and Ancient Manuscripts* (rev. ed. Harper, 1958). A classic work on a fascinating subject.

Klein, R. W. *Textual Criticism of the Old Testament.* (Fortress, 1974). Practical help for the student in applying principles and methods.

Metzger, B. M. *A Textual Commentary on the Greek New Testament* (United Bible Society, 1972). Gives reasons for textual preferences in the Society's Greek New Testament.

Dead Sea Scrolls

Cross, F. M. *The Ancient Library at Qumran:* Haskell Lectures 1956-57. (Greenwood, 1976)

Fitzmyer, J. *The Dead Sea Scrolls: Major Publications and Tools for Study* (SBL Scholars Press, 1975). An update of scholarly reference to the Dead Sea Scrolls.

Gaster, T. *The Dead Sea Scriptures* (2nd ed.) (Doubleday 1976). Translations are rather free, but one of the best books on the Dead Sea Scrolls.

Murphy, Rol. *The Dead Sea Scrolls and the Bible* (Newman, 1956). An informative paperback.

Rowley, H. *The Dead Sea Scrolls and Their Significance* (London, 1960). Popular exposition.

Vermès, G. *The Dead Sea Scrolls in English* (Pelican pb, 1968). The best English translation of the scrolls.

The Parables

Dodd, C. H. *Parables of the Kingdom* (Scribner, 1961). A fine contribution to a better appreciation of the parables.

Harrington, W. *Key to the Parables* (Paulist, 1964).

Hunter, A. M. *Interpreting the Parables* (SCM, 1960). Highly regarded.

Jeremias, J. *Parables of Jesus.* (Rev. ed., Scribner pb, 1971). A critical analysis, a return to the very words of Jesus himself. Follows Dodd in many respects.

Modern Biblical Movement

Alonso-Schokel, L. *Understanding Biblical Research* (Herder, 1963). Readable account of the biblical revival, what it is doing, and how it got where it is.

Braun, F. *The Work of Père Lagrange* (Bruce, 1963). The story of a biblical pioneer, the founder of the Ecole Biblique.

Lévie, J. *The Bible, Word of God in Words of Man* (Kenedy, 1961). Survey of the origins of the modern biblical movement.

Church Documents (N.C.W.C.)

Encyclicals: Providentissimus Deus (1893), Leo XIII
           Spiritus Paraclitus (1920), Benedict XV
           Divino Afflante Spiritu (1943), Pius XII
Biblical Commission: Letter to Cardinal Suhard of Paris, 1948.
           Intruction on the Historical Truth of the
           Gospels (1964)
Vatican II: Dogmatic Constitution on Divine Revelation (1965).

INDEX